PRAISE FOR FROM DEPTHS WE RISE

"It's one thing to talk about the moments you'll need faith the most. It's another to live through them. Sarah is someone whose story will inspire you to live your own!"
— Jon Acuff, *New York Times* Bestselling Author of *Do Over*

"Every life takes unexpected and, at times, heartbreaking turns. You will find, as I did, Sarah Rodriguez's story of heartbreak, loss, and radical hope an inspiring one."
— Stasi Eldredge, *New York Times* Bestselling Author of *Captivating* and *Becoming Myself*

"Stories are far more than just words on a page. They can be explosive agents of personal hope and transformation as you're allowed to peer into someone's most difficult moments, learning how they refused to let go. *From Depths We Rise* can be that story for all of us. Sarah Rodriguez gives a raw and intimate view of her heart as she walked through the valleys of disease, loss, death, and excruciating agony—yet still managing to emerge on the mountaintop. This inside view of her family's unfathomable journey left me forever changed."
— Christa Black Gifford, Author, Speaker, Songwriter

"People today wonder whether God is alive and still moving. Historical arguments and evidence abound that this is indeed the case, but more deeply than all of that, we want to know whether Christ is alive in us and cares about us. Sarah's story will give you hope. Her strong faith in the midst of incredibly heartbreaking circumstances will help you see that God is not only alive, but that He loves you deeply. Which is the question we're all really asking anyway."
— Carey Nieuwhof, Author and Founding Pastor, Connexus Church

"You won't be able to put this book down! Sarah's story is beautiful, tragic, faith-filled, and absolutely inspiring. This reads like a Hallmark movie, bringing every emotion you have to the surface."

A⟨…⟩ President, HomeWord, ⟨…⟩nd *Confident Parenting*

"Prepare your hea⟨…⟩ you read *From Depths We Rise*. In this p⟨…⟩hor Sarah Rodriguez brings you face-to⟨…⟩ that each of us needs to wrestle to the grou⟨…⟩ *in the middle of my pain? Is He a God of miracles or just words? Can I completely trust Him with everything that is dear to me?* This is a must-read for anyone who has ever asked these questions."
— Sherry Surratt, Director of Parenting Strategy, Orange Family Ministry, Former CEO of MOPS International, Author of *Brave Mom*

"I could not put this book down! It's a compelling story filled with a woman's courage. . . . Sarah's story will grant revived hope and faith that no matter what—God is good."

—Pam Kanaly, National Mother of Achievement,
Author of *The Single Mom and Her Rollercoaster Emotions*,
Director of Arise Ministries

"I have seen death and experienced life. There is a fine line between despair and healing and the hope that comes with that. You can feel it in Sarah's book. If you want to be encouraged and hope again, take in a deep dose of *From Depths We Rise*."

—Jeremie Kubicek, CEO & Co-Founder, Giant Worldwide,
Bestselling Author of *Leadership Is Dead* and *5 Gears*

"From Depths We Rise" is a window into an intimate struggle that will leave you breathless, yet graced with an understanding of faith only obtained in the darkest places of the human soul. What an extraordinary gift to be able to peer into the life of those who have walked through unexplainable pain and watch them emerge with such courage and purpose. For those of us who have ever uttered the words, 'it wasn't supposed to be like this,' this book is a must-read. Sarah's story will expose strength you never believed to exist, ignite even the faintest of hopes in a better tomorrow, and ultimately dare you to believe in the goodness of God. I didn't want this book to end."

—Hillary Grantham, Director, Beads of Good

"Radical people change and propel our hearts into deeper faith and joy. When you think you can't bear another sorrow of Sarah's story, she sets your heart ablaze and carries you from the ashes to a beauty and joy that transform and move you to deeper intimacy with Him. This is a story that everyone must read for this hour—it will change you forever."

—Amy Black, MA, LPC,
Director and Founder of Gold Monarch Healing Center

"I had the unique privilege of watching this painfully triumphant story be lived out in person. Sarah invites her readers into her personal journey in a refreshingly honest and hopeful way, yet she isn't afraid to wrestle with the difficult questions of life and mysterious ways of God. Her story will inspire you to keep running, to not give up, and to believe that God is truly able to make beauty from ashes."

—Chris Bennett, Lead Pastor, Antioch Norman

FROM DEPTHS WE RISE

A Journey of Beauty from Ashes

FROM DEPTHS WE RISE

SARAH RODRIGUEZ

SHILOH RUN  PRESS
An Imprint of Barbour Publishing, Inc.

Print ISBN 978-1-63409-862-5

eBook Editions:
Adobe Digital Edition (.epub) 978-1-68322-022-0
Kindle and MobiPocket Edition (.prc) 978-1-68322-023-7

Cover image: Magnolia Adams Photography

Published in association with The Blythe Daniel Agency, Inc., P.O. Box 64197, Colorado Springs, CO 80962.

Published by Shiloh Run Press, an imprint of Barbour Publishing, Inc., P.O. Box 719, Uhrichsville, Ohio 44683, www.shilohrunpress.com.

Our mission is to publish and distribute inspirational products offering exceptional value and biblical encouragement to the masses.

Member of the
Evangelical Christian
Publishers Association

Printed in the United States of America.

Acknowledgments

My Savior ~ The author of our story, my steady, my hope. That all will see.

My family ~ The constant in the storm and the piers of our foundation. We love you.

Faithful blog readers ~ My unending gratitude to everyone who has followed our story, wept for us in our grief, and rejoiced with us in our triumph. To those who have sent prayers, messages, comments, and your love, it is humbling to be a part of this community.

Joel and I were blessed to have the support of so many that loved and faithfully stood beside us as we walked through life's most trying moments. Thank you to the following families ~ Brown, Calzadilla, Cooper, Crow, Davidson, Espinoza, Forester, Franklin, Freeman, Gipson, Grantham, Hall, Hamilton, Holquin, Hopkins, Kennedy, Leach, Ley, Maulsby, Munger, Paige, Painter, Park, Perez, Peterson, Poore, Randall, Rice, Selmon, Smith, Stokes, Terndrup, Williams, Wilson, Wimer, and Wuestenfeld.

Antioch Norman ~ For the way you believed for and with us, until the very end.

Bennett family ~ The way you fight for others is beyond compare. It's an honor to do life closely together; there is no one I trust more. We love you deeply.

Much love and appreciation to our extended families ~ the Siess, Wall, Rodriguez, and Alvarez families.

To all the media outlets that told our story on a much bigger stage than we ever could've imagined ~ Thank you.

To the cancer, chemo, infertility, and PICU staffs who leaked encouragement, love, and care to our family ~ We are forever grateful.

Christa Black-Gifford, Amy and David Black, and the staff of Gold Monarch ~ For your passion to see others whole and walking in freedom. You are mending hearts and changing lives in powerful ways, mine included.

To the staff at Arise and the incredible team of writers at Anew Season ~ For the way you share of yourselves so selflessly with each and every reader.

Crio and Beads of Good ~ For sowing beauty into the darkest of places.

Magnolia Adams Photography ~ For the lovely way you choose to see the world.

Blythe ~ For your belief in me and in our story. For all the ways you made both of those things better. So thankful for you.

Kelly McIntosh and the entire staff at Barbour Publishing ~ For making this dream a reality and giving us the outlet to share our story with the world. We are forever grateful.

Kaylee ~ For the steady, faithful presence you bring to our lives. We adore you.

Lauren, Liz, Julie, Alisha, Teresa, Larissa, Lindsay, Taylor, Shyla, Stacy, Kimber, Megan, Shelly, and Hillary ~ For your deep friendship, love, and a safe place for my heart to call home.

Pierre, Jorge, Simon, and Russ ~ For the joy and friendship you brought to Joel and the beautiful ways you keep his memory alive for our children.

Lauren, Will, and Vince ~ I wouldn't have trusted anyone else to document our story. Thank you for walking this journey beside me. You have put on film what my words weren't able to capture, and it is a powerful thing. Love each of you immensely.

Milo ~ You made me a mommy and made so many of my dreams come true. You are the joy and laughter that kept me going in my darkest hour. You are brave and you are strong. You have my heart and love forever.

Ellis ~ You made me believe in the impossible again. You are the light that awakened hope in my heart and the hearts of many others. You are bold and you are mighty. You have my heart and love always.

Joel, my love ~ God is the author of our story, you are the hero of it. Your love made me come alive and is still the force that moves me forward. Your life has inspired me in ways you will never know. One day we will dance among the ruins, together.

Contents

DEDICATION

To the greatest loves my heart has ever known,
my husband and our children.

PROLOGUE

Hello, I am Sarah!"

You know when you go to an event and they have you wear those name tags with the cheesy greetings? I have never been a fan of them, mainly because they reveal so little. I am not interested in just a name but the person and his or her story.

For a long while my life was simple, textbook. I grew up in the South, or the Midwest, depending on what view you have of the US map. Most people I know use the word *y'all* if that gives you any indication. I grew up in a good home, with a good family. I went to a good school and had a lot of friends. I went on family vacations, played sports, went to the movies, and had a pretty normal adolescence. Nothing to see here, folks!

Then I got married to a wonderful man, and for a while things kept chugging along in the same normal flow I had come to know. We had the wedding and got the dog, the house, the jobs, and everything else you see people attain as they are first getting started. I was comfortable in the way I lived my life and expected life to keep moving forward the way it always had. Looking back, all the things I simply viewed as normal were gifts I didn't even know I should be thankful for until they were stripped away piece by piece.

I can even look back and see the moment when things started to turn. It started off simple enough, with a negative pregnancy test. Many women get them, right? For me it wasn't just a negative test; it was the beginning of a series of events that put me on a high-speed train toward a life that was anything but normal. Surreal might actually be a more accurate description.

From that point on, friends, even strangers, began to watch the events of our story unfold, sometimes in moments of triumph and then in moments of defeat. They have wept for us and prayed for the miraculous with us, loving my little family as if we were their own. They have seen from the outside looking in but were rarely able to understand what it feels like to be inside the story, until now.

When I first meet you, I am not only interested in the name on your name tag. I want to get in a corner with you and talk one-on-one. If time runs out on us that evening, I want to meet you later on at a coffee shop to hear even more (even though I am not a coffee drinker; I can be a walking dichotomy, I know). I want to know who you are, what makes you, you, what makes you happy and sad, what makes you tick. I want to know where you came from and where you are going. I want to understand all the little pieces that make up your puzzle. I may have seen your story from a distance, but I want to understand it up close.

So do you have some time to settle in? I have lots to tell you about me, about us, of how I journeyed from normal to a new normal. What I have to share will hopefully make you laugh—it might even make you cry—but I pray it leaves you filled with hope, because even as the story ends it is really just beginning. Sorry, I am getting a little ahead of myself. Since we are here, one-on-one, I am going to go ahead and rip off the name tag if that's okay. I have never liked those things anyway. . . .

PART I

THE DEPTHS

CHAPTER 1
First Comes Love

W hatever you do, just promise me you will not meet
a boy," my mom said earnestly.

It was an unseasonably warm January evening, and
I was out for an after-dinner walk with my mom and
sister. It was to be the last walk for the foreseeable
future. In two days I was going to pack everything I
could fit into two suitcases and board a plane for my
big move from Oklahoma to New York City. This
move was something I had been longing for, for quite
a while, but never knew quite how to make it happen.
My parents, while supportive of my dreams, were
extremely concerned at the prospect. In the end my
father had one request: if I was to move, I had to find
a job before I go. No problem. When this girl sets her
mind on something she will move heaven and earth to
make it happen. In this instance, moving heaven and
earth meant calling a woman about her receptionist job
posting and begging her to hire me over the phone. It
worked. She hired me on a Friday and asked if I could

be there on a Monday. Of course I could, I told her.

The next step was telling my parents that in seventy-two hours I would no longer be living under their roof. Instead, I would be taking everything I had to a city they'd never been to and living with people I had never met. It was definitely a sound and responsible plan. I was nothing if not determined.

I knew it wasn't boys my mom cared about. In fact, she was ready for me to find a boy, get married, and most importantly, have grandbabies. What she was not ready for was those grandbabies to be located halfway across the United States. I, on the other hand, was not in the same frame of mind. I was twenty-two years old and relishing the single life, with no significant other to worry about. I also knew that New York, though crowded, might not be the easiest city in which to meet people.

"Mom, don't worry," I replied. "The last thing I am interested in is meeting a boy."

To my surprise, a mere twelve weeks later, I met the man of my dreams. He was a tall, dark, and handsome New Yorker, the total package. A friend introduced us and arranged our first meeting, which didn't start off very smoothly. I went with him and a group of mutual friends on a trip to a large mall in West Nyack, New York. I immediately found him to be very attractive. He was gorgeous but also loud and brash, a typical New

Yorker and a total guy's guy. I, on the other hand, am a not-so-loud midwestern gal who was brought up in an entirely different environment than he.

The curt and to-the-point way in which he communicated would definitely take some getting used to. That was evident on that first day we met. Imagine my surprise that day when the first store on his agenda was Yankee Candle Company. Not only that, he seemed to be somewhat of a candle connoisseur, floating around from one candle to the next, taking in each one's scent and speaking of them in knowing terms.

I was intrigued by him and decided a little flirting might be in order—only I was terrible at it. That didn't stop me from trying.

I walked over to him, smiled coyly, and blurted out the first line that came to mind.

"Ooh, looks like you're *really* into candles, huh?"

He looked back at me, looking completely unamused and slightly annoyed. "Yeah. . .so?" he replied, sounding offended.

Hmm, I thought. *Not quite the reaction I was hoping for.*

He was obviously irritated at my flirting gone awry. I was annoyed myself and decided I didn't like him after all. Without so much as another word, I turned on my heels and left the store, trying my best to avoid him for the remainder of the day.

What had, in those moments, annoyed me completely drew me in at the same time. This guy had managed to put me in my place in an instant. Not an easy thing to do with this feisty girl.

We had the same group of friends, so I wasn't able to avoid him for long. As much as I hated to admit it, I was still pretty captivated by him. I managed to downplay it when he was around and act like I couldn't care less about his presence. He obviously wasn't interested in me, so why waste my time? Imagine my surprise when a mere three weeks later he came up to me out of the blue and asked if I would be interested in having a movie night with him.

Um. . .huh?

I was confused. I stood there for a moment formulating my response when he smiled at me—that cute, crooked, like-he-was-up-to-no-good smile. In that moment I knew I was about to dive headfirst into a relationship that would forever change my life.

I said yes to the movie night and yes to spending many more days getting to know him. Before I knew it, I had fallen in love.

ॐ

On October 16, 2004, seven months after our first meeting, Joel proposed and I accepted. We were married in Oklahoma on July 2, 2005, in front of a group of friends and family. The location was a beautiful chapel in the woods, with soaring ceilings and glass windows everywhere.

Our wedding day was magical in every way possible. I remember the poignant moments of pledging our love forever, our first kiss as man and wife where he cupped my face gently in his hands, and the joy written on both of our faces. I also remember the lighthearted moment, during our first dance, when Joel told me he was so nervous he had been downing Tums all morning long.

After our wedding we headed back to New York and to our tiny little apartment in the Bronx. Less than a year into our marriage, we were longing for a change, and more space. New York City is an incredible city to live in but an extremely hard one at that the same time. Everything was terribly expensive. Starting a family was on our mind, and we knew if we stayed we would be raising our children in a tiny apartment, lugging strollers up and down subway steps. We wanted more for ourselves than that. A move south would make it possible. Though Oklahoma certainly lacked the excitement and entertainment New York did, it gave us what we wanted in return: great jobs, a brand-new house, and stability.

We settled in easily and thrived in making our house a home. Decorating and Pier One runs became our favorite activity. We quickly made new friends and loved having them over, while our very own pampered chef, Joel, cooked us fabulous meals. Hanging out in coffee shops was a favorite pastime, especially ones that also served cupcakes. Many a Friday evening was spent cheering on Oklahoma's newly acquired NBA team and walking around downtown. Oklahoma certainly greeted us with open arms. Life couldn't get much more perfect than it already was.

∾

"So, what do you think about going ahead and trying to get pregnant?" I said to my husband in the car while driving home from a quick grocery run.

Admittedly, it was an odd time to broach such a subject, but it wasn't completely random. A journey to the back of the store to pick up an item had taken us right by the baby section. That meant we had to stroll by the land of all things teeny tiny and adorable. It wasn't as if babies weren't on our radar. It was the very reason we had moved to Oklahoma. What was holding us back was the timing.

Despite all their attempts to prevent a pregnancy, my parents had gotten pregnant with me their first month of marriage. Joel and I had a pregnancy "scare" the first month of our marriage as well. I remember the relief I felt at the negative sign on the pregnancy test. The thought of being pregnant at that time was terrifying for me. It wasn't that I didn't want to be a mom. I wanted it more than anything. It was just about finding the right moment. And at that point I didn't feel ready. I assumed getting pregnant would come easily for me. It had for my mom; why would I be any different?

That incident was a year prior. Now I was feeling more than ready. We had gotten through the adjustment first year of marriage, had relocated to a new state, and had a brand-new home and stable jobs and income. I felt there was no better time than now.

"Are you sure, babe?" my husband asked. "I mean, do you feel ready for all that comes along with a baby? Especially no sleep. I know how you like your sleep." He laughed.

"I feel ready," I said in return. "There's no better time than now. I know we've always imagined it would happen quickly, but what if it doesn't? I'm almost twenty-five, you're almost twenty-nine—at a certain point the clock starts to tick," I stated, tapping my wristwatch for dramatic effect.

"You know I've been ready for a while. If you are ready, I say we go for it. But trust me, I think it will happen quickly."

Boy, how I wish he had been right.

⁓

At the very beginning, it's not that you are *trying* to get pregnant; you are just not preventing. This is the fun part.

Your life is ripe with the possibility of what's to come. Each month could be a life-changing one, and you wait in eager anticipation for when that moment will come.

The beginning was exciting. We just *knew* we would be pregnant within the first few months. After six months, and many failed pregnancy tests, I began to wonder: *Why is this taking so long?* After nine months, an even heavier thought: *What if something is wrong with me?*

A visit to my OB showed I had a condition called polycystic ovary syndrome. While it's not anything that will prevent you from getting pregnant, it can complicate things. For me it meant an erratic monthly cycle that was hard to predict. Her recommendation was a round of fertility drugs she was fairly certain would do the trick.

One month on the drugs: nothing.

Two months on the drugs: nothing.

These drugs tend to lose their most potent effectiveness after three months. We were about to hit that mark and were perplexed at the lack of results. When my doctor recommended a surgery to go in and manually cut off the cysts from my ovaries, we jumped at the thought. The surgery would be followed by one last month of fertility drugs. Surely this was the answer, and we would finally get pregnant.

The surgery was much more invasive than I thought and required a three-day hospital stay. Joel was there with me every step of the way, sleeping on the hospital couch and helping me out of bed. It was painful, but I didn't mind taking one for the team. Joel had been tested, and nothing was wrong with his ability to produce a baby. Really, nothing was badly wrong with me. There was nothing they could see that would totally prevent us from having a child, so I believed we would have one. After the surgery I was more hopeful than ever.

Three months on the drugs, and after the surgery: nothing.

Our OB said there was no more she could do on her end and at that point recommended a fertility specialist. I wanted answers. I didn't understand why, if there were no major issues, a pregnancy wasn't happening for us. Our diagnosis of "unexplained infertility" didn't sound like a diagnosis at all. It sounded like a mockery. It was a diagnosis that said something must be happening, but we don't know exactly what.

We knew a visit to a fertility specialist would mean much more invasive measures. We were already tired physically and worn out emotionally from the last year and a half of trying. The decision was made to take a breather, some time off.

Even though we were not, at that point, using any medical measures to try to move things along, it was heartbreaking each month when we still weren't pregnant.

I had a large stash of pregnancy tests I kept under the counter. At the slightest hint of a pregnancy symptom, I would run into the bathroom and take a test. Negative, negative, negative, every time. With each negative test, my heart started to lose hope it would ever happen for us.

Then there was a glimmer of hope. We were three long years into the process when I started to develop some very strong symptoms indicating I might be pregnant. Not only that, my cycle was two weeks late. I had held off on taking a pregnancy test because I was scared—scared of another negative result and the rejection that came along with it. Finally, fifteen days after my cycle should have begun, I couldn't wait any longer. Without any fanfare, I made my way to the bathroom and pulled out another trusty pregnancy test. I took a deep breath and said a prayer.

"Please, God, let me be pregnant. I don't even care as much for myself anymore, but I want this so badly for Joel. He will make the best daddy. He wants it so badly. We have waited long enough. Please let today be the day," I whispered.

With that I took a deep breath and did the test. I put it on the counter away from my line of sight, sat on the floor, and waited the required three minutes.

When the moment finally arrived, I stood up slowly and walked over to the test.

Negative.

I had seen many negative pregnancy tests in my day, so this one shouldn't have come as a shock. But there was something about this month; it had felt like it was finally our time. It was not to be. I was so frustrated. I didn't understand why this wasn't happening for us. Sixteen-year-old girls were accidentally getting pregnant and having babies all the time. My friends were getting pregnant without even trying. People were always asking us the question "When are you two going to have a baby?" If only they knew the years and years we had been trying to no avail. It was all too much. In that moment I sank to the ground, curled into a little ball, and started to sob.

My husband ran into the bathroom to see what was wrong. He glanced at me on the ground and saw the pregnancy test on the counter, quickly putting two and two together. I was sobbing uncontrollably. He knelt down on the floor and wrapped his arms around me.

"Baby, it's okay. Don't cry."

"I can't take it anymore. I just want to have a baby. Is that too much to ask? It happens for people all the time, but not me. It's all my fault. We're not pregnant because of my stupid body not working. I just want you to be a dad. I'm so sorry you're not a dad! It's all because of me."

He looked at me in shock for the thoughts I was

thinking and the desperation I was feeling. They were words I had never voiced but that weighed heavily on my mind.

"It is not your fault at all. How can you say that?" he said.

"Because it is! If my body would just work right!" I yelled.

"None of this is your fault. I know you want this more than anything. I want this more than anything. Trust me, it will happen."

"How can you be so sure?" I replied.

"I've just always believed it will happen for us, babe. I don't know how, and I don't know when; I just know it will happen."

I wished I shared his optimism. The truth was, with each passing month I became less and less convinced. I also felt more and more like a failure. I was a woman; this was what my body was created to do, and I was failing at it miserably. I had had surgeries, taken drugs, been poked and prodded to no end, and was still no further along than I had been. I wanted to give my husband a child, make my parents grandparents. Everyone had been so hopeful and excited. It felt like I was responsible for continually dashing everyone's hopes and dreams. The amount of guilt I was feeling for it all was nearly crushing me.

I lay on that bathroom floor for quite a while. The sobs eventually stopped and turned into silent, warm tears dripping down my cheeks. My husband stayed by my side the entire time, handing me tissues and wiping the tears from my face. As I finished, he slowly pulled me to my feet and enveloped me in a huge hug. As I pulled away, he cupped my face in his hands.

"One day, you are going to be the best mom there ever was."

❦

An entire year had passed since that moment. I was now about to turn twenty-nine years old, my husband, thirty-three. We were a long time removed from that grocery store run conversation, nearly four years prior. We had never stopped trying to conceive but were still coming up empty-handed. The months once filled with anticipation for what could be were now filled with predictable dread for what I knew was to come—another month of no results. I was to the point where I was numb. I never expected it, so I didn't cry about it. The basket under my sink, once overflowing with pregnancy tests, now held a single expired test that hadn't been used in nearly a year. My heart feared I would never be able to have a child.

Since we were now many years in, with no results, we decided the time was quickly arriving that we were willing to undergo more invasive measures to get pregnant, namely, in vitro fertilization. I had done lots of studying on this procedure and knew it would be no walk in the park. Strong drugs and painful shots would be a part of my life for weeks on end. We both knew we were ready to handle it mentally but decided there were a few things we wanted to do first.

Our five-year anniversary was fast approaching, and we were dying to take a trip together. Joel, being Puerto Rican, had spent many summers there visiting family and exploring the island. He had always wanted to take me there in person, and I was game to go. We decided our fifth anniversary would be the perfect time. There was one other thing we wanted to do as well. Somehow we both got a wild hair and decided this would be a good time to try to run a half marathon. Were we runners? No. Did I enjoy running? Not in the least. A half marathon seemed like nothing that would ever be on my radar. Thirteen-point-one miles? I was currently running zero miles. Still, Joel was willing to try, and it seemed like a fun way to spend time together and also get in maximum shape before I was set to start IVF.

Our training for the half marathon was no easy feat. It required a strong time commitment and an even stronger energy commitment. We trained for four months straight, nearly every day. A few weeks before the race, I developed a hairline fracture in my hip that should've kept me from running at all. Me, being the stubborn gal I am, would not let that deter me. I had trained for this race for four long months, and darn it, I would complete it, bum hip and all.

Complete it I did. It wasn't pretty, and it wasn't terribly fast, but I conquered the race. Joel did as well, finishing about fifteen minutes ahead of me. There was incredible satisfaction in crossing the finish line. The half marathon had been a welcome distraction from all things baby. Now the race was over, and it was time to relax.

We were set to leave for Puerto Rico in six weeks; upon our return we would begin the IVF process. We were in the best shape of our lives physically and in an excellent spot emotionally, feeling refreshed, vibrant, and ready to dive back in to fertility treatments. Life was hopeful, even joyous again at what was to come. Then, in an instant, it all came crashing down.

∽

"Babe, something weird just happened," Joel said to me as he walked into our bedroom.

I was lying in bed watching TV. Exhausted from a full day of work, this was one of my few moments to unwind before I went to bed.

"What?" I asked, barely turning my attention away from the television show I was watching.

"I just went to the bathroom, and there was blood in

my urine," he said.

I looked away from the TV. Seeing the anxiety in his face, I immediately went into downplay mode.

"Don't worry about it, honey. It's probably just a bladder infection or something."

"Yeah, you're probably right," he conceded.

My husband is more of a "go to a doctor and get a prescription" kind of person. I am more of a "take extra vitamin C and a nap and feel better in the morning" type of person. Our first response was just to wait it out and see if it got any better. It didn't. In fact, a few days later the blood returned, only now there was so much of it. It turned the entire toilet bowl a bright shade of red. We both decided it was time to get this checked out with our family doctor.

Joel went to his appointment, calling me as soon as he got out. He said they had mentioned getting a CT scan but changed their mind to just a round of antibiotics. They assumed it was either a bladder infection or kidney stones. If it was a bladder infection, it would clear up with the antibiotics. If not, then Joel would have to undergo a CT scan, which would more than likely reveal the presence of kidney stones. I was immediately relieved. A bladder infection was no big deal. I had dealt with kidney stones before myself, and while extremely painful, they were something that we could deal with.

My relief was short lived.

᷈

"Something's wrong." Joel came into the living room and said a week later.

This time I looked at his face—sheer panic. He was almost on the verge of tears.

After he had taken the antibiotics for an entire week, the blood had seemed to go away. We thought everything was fine.

"What's going on?" I asked him.

"I just peed, and a blood clot came out."

"What?" *This is strange,* I thought. "Can you show me?"

He walked me over to our bathroom and pointed. There, sitting in the toilet, about the size of a large dried plum, was a blood clot. The entire toilet was stained bright red.

I looked at his face. The fear was evident. Now I needed to talk him down, tell him everything was going to be okay. Only I wasn't so sure it was. I was scared myself.

"Call the doctor first thing Monday morning. I am sure it's just kidney stones. It is going to be okay."

"All right," was his quiet reply.

That night I did something I shouldn't have. I went online and typed in "blood in urine." It gave a huge number of responses to what it could be, from the small to the large. It mentioned kidney stones, but to my horror, it mentioned another possibility. Cancer. I briskly shut down my computer, brushing away the thought. *I am sure everything is fine,* I kept telling myself. Everything had to be fine. The truth was, I wasn't so sure.

ᘓ

Joel went back to the doctor, who immediately ordered a CT scan for the next day. I went with him. As soon as he was finished, a nurse came out and told him they wanted him to do another scan, this time with contrast. I thought it was a little odd but didn't dwell on it. Truth is, we were more concerned about our car possibly being pummeled by a rapidly approaching hailstorm. They quickly finished up the additional scan and gave us an appointment time to meet with our doctor the next morning for results. Finally finished, we ran to our car and raced home, just beating the large storm. We were in the thick of tornado season, and tornadoes were nothing out of the ordinary for our state. The weather that evening turned chaotic, and we spent much of that evening in our closet, with tornadoes roaring by only a few miles up the road.

That next morning we left work early to visit with the urologist for the results of the scan. On the thirty-minute drive to the doctor's office, we were both abnormally quiet, lost in thought. I remember looking up at the bright blue sky and thinking how beautiful the weather was that day. How crazy it was that one night you could be taking cover from a tornado and the next morning admiring creation in the form of a gorgeous blue sky. Life can drastically change from one moment to the next. If there was anything I knew from the previous battles I had faced, it was the ups and downs that life contains. Disappointments had taught me that joy could be interrupted by sorrow, yet sorrow can be snuffed out by joy.

While the thought seemingly came from nowhere, I believe it was God preparing my heart for the earth-shattering news we were moments away from receiving. It was the calm before the storm. I couldn't put my finger on exactly what was about to happen, but I couldn't shake the feeling that life was about to change. Drastically. I tried to steady myself and prepare my heart for what that just might be. I felt the uneasiness penetrating my entire body, and it frightened me. For my husband's sake, I tried to clothe myself in strength, yet on the inside I was begging for peace.

∽

We arrived at the doctor's office and were quickly rushed back to a small room to await the results. We waited and waited. Finally a nurse popped her head in to say the doctor was reading the scan now and should be back in about five minutes. Only it wasn't five minutes. Five minutes became thirty minutes. As time wore on, my worry began to grow. What was going on?

We heard the small, quick knock at the door signaling the doctor's impending entrance. *Finally,* I thought.

The doctor walked in and noticed me.

"Well, I remember you," he said to me weakly.

"Yeah. . ." I laughed. "Kidney stones," I said with a smile to the doctor who had been my savior two years prior when I was sick with the painful stones.

He did not smile back. He looked straight to my husband.

"Sir, you have kidney cancer," he said bluntly.

What? Time stood still. Like the cliché everyone says, it really does feel like a bad dream. All at once I felt confused, dizzy, and disoriented. It was as if the room were closing in on me. I struggled to stand. I kept waiting for the doctor to say, "Just kidding," as sick as that would be. He never did.

"There is a large mass on your left kidney. It has been growing for quite some time."

I looked at Joel. He looked down to the floor and back at the doctor again. He didn't say a word, shed a tear, or show emotion. He was blank.

"I'm sorry," the doctor said. "When we asked you to go get a CT scan, we never in a million years would have guessed it was this. You are so young and healthy."

He was right. Joel was in his early thirties and had never been healthier. He had just trained for and completed a half marathon and lost forty pounds doing so.

I didn't know what to do. I rose from my chair, stood beside Joel, and began to rub his back. He looked at me, giving me a slight smile as if to reassure me. I felt like I had been punched in the gut. All these thoughts came at me in full force. You hear the word *cancer* and automatically think of it as a death sentence.

You will never be a mom like you had dreamed. You are going to be a widow in your twenties. You will have to deal with life without your best friend. What are you going to do? The thoughts were assaulting me left and right. I couldn't let it show.

They took us to another room and showed us the CT scan pictures of the nearly seven-pound tumor in my husband's abdomen. As my legs started to give out, someone shoved a chair underneath me. Tissues magically appeared in my hand. I couldn't believe what I was seeing.

The doctor cleared his throat and told us the survival rate would be fifty-fifty. How did we wake up this morning and get dressed for work like any other day, and now here we were talking about survival rates for my husband? This was unreal.

I finally cleared my head enough to gather the questions I wished to ask.

"Will he lose his kidney?"

"Absolutely," the doctor said. "It is totally engulfed by

the cancer. He has more than likely been functioning off one kidney for quite a while."

"How long do you think he has had the cancer?"

"If I had to guess. . . ," he speculated, "years."

"I am a visual person," I told him. "What are we talking about sizewise? Like the size of a golf ball?"

He paused and then ever so slowly stated, "More like the size of a football."

We sat stunned. There was nothing more to say.

We left the room and walked past the front desk as another group of nurses gave condolences with their eyes as we passed.

Tears poured down my face as we held hands and walked to our car.

I turned to Joel. "We are going to beat this, JoJo," I told him.

He nodded a weak yes.

"Joel, we are going to beat this," I stated again. "There are plenty of people who get this news and it turns out okay. You are going to live. We are going to make it through this."

The shock was evident on his face as he slowly, yet silently, nodded in agreement.

CHAPTER 2
Not Again

We walked slowly hand in hand down the beach, soft sand under our toes and waves breaking at our feet. The sun was setting, painting the sky a beautiful haze of deep oranges, purples, and pinks. Life was good. We were a few months removed from the most difficult year of our life. Joel had been through a surgery to remove the kidney and the cancer that had engulfed it. A year of intense chemo followed, along with flights back and forth to be monitored at a top cancer hospital in Houston, Texas.

He was recently given a clean bill of health and told the cancer was in remission. It had been a long road, but we were celebrating its end. We believed cancer was firmly behind us.

Many asked us how we got through this time of such hardship. Well, it wasn't easy. Cancer tests every bit of endurance you have within you. It places a strain on every area of your life, but the area it attacks relentlessly is your faith. Questions abounded inside as to why we had to walk this road, and fatigue set in when we felt we couldn't do it alone. That is when we realized we weren't doing it alone. Looking back, we lovingly referred to the days of cancer as the best worst days of our life because as difficult as they were, they were the moments that changed us forever in the loveliest ways. It caused us to cling to each other like never before. Even more so, it caused us to cling to the Lord like never before. In these moments He wasn't just words on a page, or a God in the heavens. He was Father, He was friend, He was grace, He was strength. He was all we needed.

In a practical sense, though, life would *never* return to "normal." We found ourselves settling back into a routine. Joel was now employed again at the company where we both worked and was set to begin work in a few weeks. He was elated. We were celebrating our victory by taking the trip to Puerto Rico that had been derailed by the cancer. Ever since we first met, he had told me he couldn't wait to take me one day. It didn't disappoint. We lay by the beach sunning and eating to our hearts' content. One of my favorite days was spent walking the cobbled streets of Old San Juan taking pictures of landmarks. We went to the bio bay, went snorkeling, and spent the day on a catamaran. The most favorite landmark of Joel's was the El Morro Fort, or as he simply called it, "The Fort." As a child this was one of his favorite places to go and explore. We even have a sassy picture of him posing there in all his 1980s glory.

"When we have a baby we *totally* have to bring him to this fort one day," he told me.

His eyes were lit up like a Christmas tree that trip, not only because of where we were but also because of what was just around the corner. We had decided once we returned from our trip we were going to go back to the fertility clinic and use the sperm we had stored to finally start our family. Knowing chemo could render a man sterile, we made the choice pre-chemo to have some frozen. We didn't know it then, but it was a decision that would change our lives and allow us the option to start a family quickly after cancer.

Our plans had been on pause for a year, and we didn't want to wait any longer to start our family. I was apprehensive. I knew IVF could be a complicated process and didn't always work. Joel couldn't be convinced otherwise.

"It's going to work, baby," he would smile and tell me. "Really, it is. Trust me."

He was right.

∼

Two months later, after a long, difficult round of IVF, we got the phone call with the news we had been waiting five years to receive.

"Congratulations, you are pregnant!"

I couldn't believe our dream had finally come true. We were going to be parents. All the years of dreaming of this moment, praying, begging, standing, and now our promise had come. To a new child entering the world I would be known as "Mommy" and my husband as "Daddy." Our own little family was being created just as we had always wanted. We had endured a lot of pain to arrive here, but every bit of it was now worth it. I never knew if I would have this opportunity to love someone greater than myself and Joel. My heart was so very thankful for this gift—the gift of life.

Two weeks later we were at the doctor's office, having an ultrasound performed, when we received even better news.

"What would you think about having twins?" the doctor said with a huge smile on his face.

"Are you serious?" I exclaimed.

"Well, I wouldn't joke about something like that," he said wryly.

I looked at Joel and laughed at the shocked expression on his face. He recovered quickly, and his shock turned to sheer joy.

We walked hand in hand to the car with the ultrasound pictures in tow. We had left many a doctor's visit hand in hand in tears, but now we were leaving with hearts exploding with happiness. Not only one baby, but two. We could barely contain our excitement.

"Twins," Joel kept saying over and over again, shaking his head in elated disbelief.

⤳

For ten glorious weeks I would hold on to my belly and talk to my babies—the babies we had prayed for and pleaded for—and the fact that they were here seemed beyond belief. I would wake up in the night to pray for these babies, pleading with God to keep them healthy and safe. As mothers of twins will tell you, the two babies sometimes start to take on the identity of one. Yes, they are separate individuals, but they come together as one glorious, breathtaking package. And from the very first moment, I loved and wanted both of them with every last fiber of my being.

When I was eleven weeks pregnant we went for a routine ultrasound. We were one week away from getting through the first trimester, breathing a sigh of relief, and sharing our amazing news with the world. The doctor came in, said hello, and got to work. I turned my head to the right to look at the screen. I immediately saw my first precious baby. Wow, how he had grown! In just a few weeks he had gone from a small little bean to now looking like a real baby. I saw his little heart beating. Relief. The doctor moved the wand around, looking for the second baby. He looked.

He looked. The room was silent. Too silent.

He turned to me and said, "Well, I am sure you have heard of a vanishing twin. This is common in IVF."

In that moment I knew exactly what he meant. My two babies had now become one baby. I felt slow tears rolling down my face as the nurse handed me a tissue.

"It's okay," the doctor said. "It really is better this way. A single pregnancy will be better on you and your baby than a twin one would've been."

What? How on earth could he say such a thing? I had fought so long and so hard for these babies. *Both* were loved. *Both* were wanted. My life never seemed to take the easy route to get anywhere. It didn't matter to me how hard a twin pregnancy would be. From the moment I heard two heartbeats, I was ready to move heaven and earth to hold two lives in my arms. I felt like the Lord had doubled our blessing. Now it felt as if half of it was being cruelly ripped away.

He tried in vain to make me realize what a fabulous consolation prize I had won, yet I was unmoved.

Sensing my sorrow, he stiffly patted me on the leg and exited the room quickly, letting me fall apart alone.

The room was empty. My heart was empty. I started to dress, as Joel sat silently, not knowing what to say. In that moment I wept. In the hours to come I wept. In the days to come I wept. Vanish—how could my baby just vanish, my child I had wanted more than anything in my life? It was growing, it was developing, its heart was beating, and now it was gone.

Before we left, the doctor explained to us that this was normal and many times both twins weren't strong enough to make it on their own so one twin would give its life so the other could grow. My precious little hero baby.

I would never get to see my baby on this earth. I would never get to hold him in my arms. I would never get to throw him a birthday party or shower his cheeks with kisses. The promise of knowing I would see him one day didn't change how badly I was already missing him now. Life had seemed unfair before, but this seemed so very senseless. My heart was heavy with loss. The pain I felt over my child I had never really known took my breath away. Life would find a way to move forward, as it always does, but there would always be something missing because *someone* was.

༄

In the days to come, I was a wreck. I fell into a dark place. From the moment of conception, it was always two babies in my mind. They were separate but they were one, a package deal, each wanted. All my hopes and dreams for my two babies were now being consolidated to one child, and it just didn't feel right. In losing one, it felt like I had lost them both. Since death had visited me, it felt like all the life had left as well. How could grief and joy coexist?

It felt wrong to be happy for my child who remained, yet it felt wrong not to be happy for my child that remained. I wanted to honor my loss, but deep down I knew I couldn't do it by refusing all joy and choosing sorrow. I didn't know how I would, but I knew we are to honor death by living life. By trading our ashes for beauty. By trading our mourning for joy. By choosing to rise. For me, there was no other choice.

Six nights later we attended Christmas Eve service at our church. We came home, and I sat down in the chair. I felt something wet. I shouldn't be feeling anything wet. I went to the bathroom. Blood was pouring out of my body and was all over my clothes. Blood, bright red blood; I will never forget the sight. After the ultrasound the doctor told me in the case of vanishing twins you won't bleed, and if I did I should immediately go to the hospital. This wasn't just light bleeding—this was everywhere, and it was so frightening.

In that moment I felt like I had just lost the second baby. My empty heart now felt even emptier; all those days of IVF shots, doctor's appointments, ultrasounds, tears, prayers, all for nothing. My loss didn't just entail one child; my body was now getting rid of the second one as well.

I screamed for Joel. He ran into the bathroom and saw the blood. He went silent.

"I'm miscarrying the second baby," I stated, as plainly as I would state that I am done with my plate. I sounded numb; I felt numb.

"What do we do?" he asked.

"We need to go to the ER," I responded.

He knelt down beside me and assured me no matter what, everything was going to be okay. I didn't believe him.

We loaded up in the car and headed to the ER. As we walked through the doors, the waiting room was empty. Why would it be full? It was Christmas Eve. People were supposed to be at home celebrating with their families, not sitting in a stark room with broken hearts and streaming tears.

They took me to a room, took my vitals, took blood, asked questions. . .and more questions. . .and more questions. . . . They told me the doctor would be there in a moment to do my ultrasound. A few moments later, he was there, and so was the jelly as he moved the wand around.

And then I saw it, a small flicker of light.

Boom, boom, boom.

A heartbeat. I could hardly believe my eyes. My child. My one remaining child still lived. He hadn't left us like his brother or sister had. He was there, he was alive, and he was strong. Relief washed over every part of me. With each beat of his heart, mine was filling with hope again—hope that this baby's life was just beginning and would grow into all that the Lord had for him—hope that he was still being formed and fashioned, and one day his great purpose would be fulfilled on this earth with me by his side. We weren't going to have to say good-bye; one day we would get to say hello.

Two days later we had one more ultrasound in our doctor's office where he confirmed our sweet baby was still alive in my womb. The baby was measuring correctly, moving all around, and even appeared to wave to us. In an instant, everything changed. I went from total despair and indifference to wanting this baby with all I had. It snapped me from depression and made me realize how hard I needed to fight to bring this baby into the world. I had felt the sting of the punch, but I would not stay down. The depths would not take anything more than they already had. I had so deeply wanted life, and I would fight for it with all I had.

The doctor said everything looked great and I should carry the baby to term. My, what this child had made it through to get to us. He was a fighter. We didn't know the gender yet, but I told Joel he would be a boy named Milo—our little soldier.

Our hearts were broken for the child we lost, but a

blessing still remained in my womb. For that we were so very thankful.

꧁

We could not be more thrilled to finally be pregnant. This had been a dream of both of ours since the beginning of our marriage. So many times it looked like it might remain just that—a dream. We had been dealt such a bad hand, but finally it appeared to be turning around. Joel was thrilled the entire pregnancy. He would laugh with delight when we would see our ultrasound pictures, and he would talk to my belly endlessly. He doted on me and made sure to take care of my every need so I could get rest. It was definitely some of the happiest nine months of our life together. We were thrilled to be done with cancer and chemo and ready to move on to the amazing life that we had in store. For ones who had been through so much, we were finally feeling blessed and like things were turning around for our good. Our family had walked through tragedy and loss and the winding road of disappointment that life had not gone as planned. Never would we stop moving forward and seeking to conquer all that life had thrown our way. We believed we had seen the worst of it. We had lived in the depths of despair, and it finally seemed as if we were able to breathe again.

And then...

We went in to the doctor's office for one of Joel's

routine appointments. Every time before these appointments, I would get knots in my stomach. When you have been dealt such devastating blows in the past, it is normal to brace yourself for it to possibly happen again. What wasn't normal was the fact I was now six months pregnant and in full waddle glory as we walked into the doctor's office. The most excruciating part is waiting for the doctors to come into the room. When they finally do enter, they have a poker face. You can't really tell what's coming. But in a moment, it all became clear.

"I am going to do a small physical examination of you," the doctor said. "Can you breathe in and out?"

She asked Joel to take deep breaths, then small ones, then deep ones. Over and over again she examined his lungs, moving around her stethoscope. She finally finished and looked at the ground. I knew what was coming next. I braced myself and held my breath.

"On your CT I am noticing a few areas of concern on your lungs."

No, no, no, *no*! An area of concern. I knew what that meant. They thought the cancer had returned—not in his kidney area, but this time spreading to his lungs.

Joel looked over at me. I immediately put my hand on my belly and looked to the floor to try to keep the tears from pouring down my face. Not now. It couldn't happen now. We thought we were done with cancer. We were pregnant with our first child and about to move into our newly built home. If there was ever a time when this should not happen, it was now.

I continued to look at the floor as she talked with Joel. Right now the areas of concern were so small that they were not able to be biopsied yet. The best course of action was to wait ten weeks and then come back and get another CT scan to see if the areas had grown. From there, he would have a biopsy to confirm if it was cancer. With that timeline, it put all of this happening right around my due date. Talk about bad timing. I was dumbfounded. We politely thanked the doctor, made our follow-up appointment, and walked to the car.

Joel sat down in his seat, quiet. I knew what he was thinking. He had waited so very long for this moment in his life—to have a home, a job he loved, and a family that he adored. Was he going to get all these things only to not be there to enjoy them? For once neither of us had any words. We had beaten this disease once. How would we fight it again? Why now? This was supposed to be our time of joy after heartache. Hadn't we endured enough?

He looked at me and saw the tears trickling down my face as I once again subconsciously rubbed my belly.

"You know it's going to be okay, right? It has to be a glitch on the CT scan. It just has to be. I feel fine. There is no way I have cancer again. I promise you, it will be fine," he said.

I nodded slowly and even managed to get out a small smile. While I acted like I agreed, I didn't. Deep down in my heart, I knew the cancer had returned. Call it a gut feeling or just someone who knew that life can be wildly unpredictable, if not unfair. As much as I wanted it to be nothing, the Lord was preparing my heart for the worst. We had another battle on our hands.

The next ten weeks passed rather quickly. I was in the last trimester of pregnancy. We moved into our new home, had multiple baby showers, and prepared to meet our new baby boy. It wasn't that we didn't know what we were facing—it was the unspoken shadow in the corner of the room. We had just waited so long for this moment in our lives, and we were determined to forge ahead, hope for the best, and live in hopeful anticipation for what was to come. Maybe it was all just a mistake in the scans. Maybe it was nothing. Truth is, we didn't know, and we wouldn't for a while. In the next ten weeks, there was nothing that could be done about it, so we made a choice to try our best to enjoy these last few weeks as a family of two while gearing up to become a family of three. While we certainly weren't pretending to know or even understand why this was happening (and why it was happening now), we made the choice to trust. Yes, I was always afraid of losing my husband, but it just seemed as if our battle couldn't possibly end that way. We had conquered so much. There was no reason to believe the Lord would not continue to fight on our behalf.

Before we knew it, the time had come. It was time for our follow-up appointment for Joel. We walked into the doctor's office, where they told us news that was not surprising but very devastating. The areas of concern had grown since the last scan, and the doctors were now 90 percent sure this was a cancer reoccurrence. There we were again, in a delicate dance between sorrow and joy. On one hand our dreams were coming true; on the other hand, our fears were coming true. It was as if our lives were a rip current. Each time we would manage to find our way to the surface, an unseen force was pulling us into the depths over and over again. It was unrelenting and exhausting.

They scheduled Joel a biopsy for the following Tuesday. My due date was Friday. This was the worst possible timing. We were trying to remain excited about the birth of our son, but this dark cloud was looming ahead. It was hard to feel excited about our future when there were so many scary unknowns about just what exactly that future entailed. We were being pulled out further into the sea and clinging to each other like never before.

The morning of the biopsy arrived. We walked into

the hospital holding hands. I was wearing one of the only dresses that fit and a pair of flip-flops on my swollen feet. As I sat back in the surgical waiting room with Joel, I was physically uncomfortable from my pregnancy, but more than that, I was incredibly nervous about what these tests would reveal. Nurses walked by and would look in, see me, and smile. I could tell their smiles were half-pity. They all knew what Joel was there for, and seeing a hugely pregnant wife with him seemed to have a sobering effect on everyone in that room, myself included.

I believe firmly that coincidences are God's way of manifesting Himself to show we are never alone. We had many "coincidences" we encountered during this journey, and that day was no different. The nurse who was taking care of Joel was asking about his story. He shared it from start to finish as she listened and nodded.

After he finished, she told him, "Joel, do not give up hope." She continued, "I have had cancer that has jumped around to three different places in my body. I have had surgery, and I have had chemo many times over. But I will never stop fighting and never give up hope, and neither should you."

I turned to look at my husband. He had always had a fighting spirit in him, but he was now nodding vigorously. I knew there was no doubt he would fight, and at the moment I had no doubts that he would beat it. No, it was not the audible voice of the Lord telling me it would be okay. Rarely is it ever. It was more like a still, small voice inside, telling me to continue to trust. To rest in hope.

They took Joel to the back room for a quick biopsy, telling him to call our doctor on Friday, my due date. The results would be in by then. But a little something happened before we could get to Friday. I just so happened to go into labor.

It was Thursday, the day before my due date, July 5. I started to feel intense contractions on my way to work. Since I'd had so many false labor alarms, I didn't think this could possibly be the real deal. I told Joel to go ahead and drop me off at work and I would time my contractions for an hour and see where I stood. I sat there at my desk in extreme pain, breathing through my contractions and timing them via an app on my phone. An hour later on the dot, I picked up the phone to call Joel.

"Um, honey?" I started in.

"Yes, what's up?" he answered breathlessly.

"I timed my contractions for an hour, and they are averaging two minutes apart. . . ." I trailed off.

"*What!*" was his high-pitched reply. "I will be right there!"

Right there he was, the entire time. When we got to

the hospital, he made a big deal of getting a wheelchair and wheeling me up to my room. I took the easy way out and went ahead and got the epidural. From the moment they gave it to me, I instantly relaxed. I was as calm as could be, and Joel, my family, and I sat and watched HGTV for eight hours until they came in and told me it was time to push. Joel held my hand but mostly stayed quiet. That was on my direction. I had playfully said to him one time, "Don't you dare tell me that I'm [air fingers] 'doing great' while I'm pushing. I just might break your hand." He gave me a look that said duly noted. When the time came, his presence by my side was all the help that I needed.

Finally, the long-awaited moment arrived when we got to meet the baby we had dreamt of for so long. He was a stout eight-pound, eight-ouncer with lots of dark hair, beautiful in every way. His cry was magic. It was amazing all the things he went through during the pregnancy to get to us. He was a little soldier for sure, the meaning of his name held true. Milo Andrew Rodriguez, our most perfect gift.

As they were cleaning me up, I had my eyes fixed on Joel. He was absolutely smitten and completely in awe of this new life. He kept going back and forth between checking on Milo and checking on me. In that moment, what was to come in the days ahead didn't matter, and neither did what had transpired in our family with Joel's cancer. We had our family, and life couldn't get any better. I only wish in the midst of our joy there wasn't a lingering apprehension for our future. The purity of the moment as it should have been was robbed from us as we knew in our gut we might not receive the good news we were hoping for from Joel's biopsy.

The next day was Friday morning. Joel had slept at the hospital with me, and Milo had done an excellent job sleeping his first night in the world. As I sat on the bed, Joel was holding Milo in his arms, smiling and taking phone pictures. I didn't know if he had forgotten what day it was.

"Joel, you know it's Friday, right?" I started in hesitantly.

"I know," he said, not taking his eyes off Milo.

"I'm sure those results will be ready by now if you want to call," I said.

"Babe, do you think it would be okay if we wait until Monday to find out?"

I knew what he was thinking. He was hoping for the best but realistically preparing for the worst. Even in this moment of sheer bliss, holding and taking in the beauty of our son, cancer was intruding on us like a dark cloud. It still makes me angry to this day that we were both having to bear the weight of such a heavy load.

"Yes, baby. Let's just wait until Monday." I sighed and went back to looking at my son's gorgeous little face.

〰️

Our first weekend home was a blur of activity. Diapers, feedings, burpings, sleepless nights—repeat. We were in the haze of new parenthood, filled with wonder at the life God had entrusted to us. We cooed at our perfect baby, dreaming together about snow cone stand runs with our boy, evenings spent at Little League games, movie nights as a family, and exploring the world together. There was talk of many future things but never about what was right around the corner that following Monday.

It came far too quickly. This time they didn't wait for us to call; the doctor called us. Joel went to the master bathroom for privacy. I gave the baby to my mom and followed him in. He looked up at me as if he wanted to protect me but was grateful for my support at the same time. I sat quietly on my bed and stared at the fibers of my comforter listening to him.

"Yes. Yes. Okay. Yes. Um-hmm. Oh. . .it is. . ."

Joel looked over to me as he slowly nodded his head yes. The cancer was back. Floods of tears slipped down my cheeks, so I left the room and sat on the couch to let him finish talking to the doctor.

"It's back, Mom. It's back," I said to her as the sobs started to spill out of my body.

She came and handed me my son. My little baby boy.

He was sleeping so peacefully in my arms, completely unaware of the chaos around him. As I looked at him, a million thoughts filled my head. *Will he have his father in his life? Will his father get to watch him grow? Will I be raising him alone? How will I ever do this alone?*

Joel came out of the room, his face white. My heart was aching and broken for him. This should have been one of the happiest, most carefree moments of his life, and once again cancer took that from him and also our entire family. I got up from the couch and hugged him. I didn't know what to say other than it was going to be okay. He looked in my eyes and looked at our son. Joel had lost both his parents to cancer. I knew that thought was never far from his mind, especially now as a new parent. Milo upped the ante. He was now our reason to fight harder than ever before.

"Yes, babe, it will be okay," he said.

In that moment joy was continuing to battle sorrow as fear took the throne from peace. We had been here before—too many times before. Every time hope began to rise, we were pulled deeper into the depths. And on this day—well, we just wanted to pretend that life couldn't possibly be that cruel again.

The very next day Joel underwent a surgery to have a chemo port put back in. The worst part was since it was in his chest, he was not allowed to do anything strenuous. That meant that for two days he could not hold our son. When you wait nine months to finally meet this amazing little person, all you want to do is hold him. I absolutely could not imagine being told I could not hold my child. I always tried to be strong, but that week I allowed the tears to freely flow. I was sad for my husband for what he had to walk through. I was angry at this stupid disease for constantly wreaking havoc on our lives. I was still tired from the last battle and unsure about how we would go through this all again. I was scared at what we had in front of us and what the future would hold. While the early moments with Milo held joy for our family, stress, fear, and heartache were equally present in our lives.

⁓

The very next week after that, Joel started his second course of chemo. It was really different this time. The first time it was just him and me. I never missed a chemo appointment or a doctor's appointment. This time I had a brand-new baby, and as much as Joel needed me, Milo did, too. Joel did his best to relieve me of the burden.

"I am going to be fine," he said to me through tears. "I have been through this before, I know what to expect, and I will be fine to go alone. Trust me, the most important thing you can do for me right now is take care of our son. He needs you."

"But you need me, too, JoJo!" I said.

I felt pulled in two different directions at once, yet there was only one of me. In the end someone was going to get less of me, and we both knew it. In true Joel fashion, he wanted to make sure his wife and son were taken care of, number one and number two. That left him as number three. Slowly I started to understand this is just how it would have to be. I would not be able to be at every single chemo treatment, and there might be a doctor's appointment I would have to miss every now and then. Our biggest priority had to be our son, taking care of him, and making him feel loved and secure. I didn't want cancer to compromise his first year of life any more than it already had.

Joel made the decision for us that he would do chemo treatments on his own this time while I watched the baby. For doctor's appointments we would find someone to watch Milo, and I would go along for support. Another decision Joel made was to keep this quiet from his work. He wanted to continue working while doing chemo. He had only been back on the job a year at that point, and he didn't want to lose it. He wanted to continue to help provide for his family. I tried over and over again to talk him out of it. I told him that we would be fine if he went on disability again. We could find a way to make ends meet. I had respected this man before, but seeing his determination to beat cancer again while working so hard took my admiration to a completely different level. He was unrelenting. God had given me the man of my dreams and my son the most amazing father. My greatest fear was that Joel would get everything he ever wanted in life but not be here to live it out. I could not imagine my life without this man, and I didn't want to.

We told very few people the cancer had returned—only family and close friends. He kept his secret close to the vest. We were going to have to battle it out again for his life, but we were determined to continue to live our life in the process. Cancer had taken too much already, and we were determined not to let it take away everything we had. We tried our best to enjoy our baby while also fighting for Joel's life. It wasn't easy.

One moment we would be laughing at the silly face my son would make, and in the next my eyes would fill with tears at the thought of all we were facing. One moment I was confident the Lord would swoop in and save the day, and the next I feared He was not even hearing my prayers. It was a merry-go-round of emotions—up, down, round and round. Never before had I known so much heartache, yet so much joy, could exist all at once.

CHAPTER 3
Time Stands Still

My nerves threatened to overtake me as I walked into our doctor's office to get results from Joel's most recent scans. He had endured chemo all the way from August until January. We would continue to go in for scans every other chemo round, delighted to see with each scan the tumor was shrinking more and more. Joel continued to work despite the fact he was undergoing very difficult treatments. We still kept what we were walking through quiet, trying desperately to enjoy our time with our new son. By the time February rolled around, the tumor in his lung had shrunk down to where it was no longer visible. Our doctor recommended we take a three-month break to see how Joel's body would respond.

Taking a break? No complaints from us! I thought.

We used that time to be a family in the way that you should be together the first month of your child's life. We even took a family trip to Colorado, one of our favorite places on the planet. We also dramatically cleaned up Joel's diet and tried any and every natural remedy we could find that might be helpful.

We had been having such an amazing time together without the threat of cancer. I wanted nothing more than to stay in our perfect little bubble we had created, even though I knew it was impossible. Life had to return to normal at some point. Our normal just so happened to be a constant state of wait and see.

Soon the break was over and we sat in the hospital room in complete silence, waiting for the doctor to arrive. Our glorious break from reality had come to an abrupt end as we steeled ourselves for the news of what our fate would be.

The only sound was the nervous tapping of Joel's foot on the linoleum floor and the crinkling sounds the paper made underneath him as he shifted back and forth. The doctor walked in the room. One look at his face and I knew it wasn't going to be good.

"So we have some growth in the tumor size from the last scan," he said.

"When you say *growth*, what do you mean?" I asked.

"Well, when I say growth, I mean it has grown back to the size it was pre-chemo."

We were dumbfounded. In the three months we had taken a break, this tumor had grown back to a size that negated the five months of chemo Joel had endured. We felt like we were kicked in our guts again. All we wanted was freedom from sickness and our lives back again.

Instead we were told all of his hard work did absolutely nothing.

The doctor told us at this point he wanted to move to a different course of action. Instead of chemo he wanted to go in and surgically remove the tumor. I was immediately hesitant. Once you go in and start poking around, the cancer can do unpredictable things. I was also concerned with putting Joel's body through yet another major surgery only three years out from the first one and after enduring almost a year and a half total of chemo.

The room fell silent. I said the words that I knew Joel was thinking but too afraid to say.

"Doctor, at this point are we just buying time, or do you really believe he can beat this?"

It may have sounded abrupt, but we needed to know. I didn't want my husband to continue to endure procedure after procedure only to put him through something that wouldn't save his life in the end.

"I think he can still beat it," was his reply. "I really do."

One thing I did know was there was no one more determined to beat this disease than my precious husband.

We spent the next several weeks in a tailspin in meetings with specialists and the surgical team. We finally told Joel's boss, who was shocked he was able to keep this quiet for so long, never even calling in sick once. We sought the advice of friends and family and prayed really, really hard. During those next few weeks, it became more and more difficult for Joel to breathe as the tumor grew larger in his chest. Breathing in and out is something we all take for granted until lung cancer makes it a laborious activity. We finally decided, despite our extreme hesitancy, moving forward with the surgery was our only option. We called the doctor, who gave us a surgery date for the following week.

"I was thinking," Joel started in, "if they cut me open on my chest to get to my lung, that means that at least for a few weeks I won't be able to rock Milo to sleep, right?"

Up to this point we each had our "duties," so to speak, of who would handle what in regard to our son. Joel's duty had always been to give Milo his evening bottle and rock him to sleep. He had been the main one who would do so every single night, chemo or no chemo. There would be nights he would come home sick as a dog and I would say, "Maybe I should just rock Milo tonight?" He would say no—adamant it would be him. Those were his most special times with his son, and there was nothing he treasured more. I looked at him and gave my answer.

"No, honey, you probably won't be able to for a while."

Silent but steady tears started to pour down his face and, in turn, mine, too.

⁓

Neither of us slept the night before surgery. Still, we had been reassured this would be a fairly straightforward procedure. Joel would be in for about a weeklong hospital stay and a two-week recovery time. This delighted us because it meant he would be healed up and able to attend our son's first birthday party extravaganza, a party I had embarrassingly been planning for half of his life. Our sitter arrived early, and it was time to go. I went back to our son's room to find Joel sitting in the rocker, talking to Milo and giving him kisses.

"Daddy's going to be gone for a while and I will miss you *so, so* much, but I will be home very soon, okay, buddy? You take care of Mommy while I'm gone. I love you, bud." It melted my heart and still does as I think about it.

I grabbed my cell phone and instinctively took a picture of both of them—Milo in his PJs, completely oblivious to the impending situation, and Joel already wearing a medical bracelet and looking apprehensive. A father holding the long-awaited gift of his son. Life was about to radically change. Our story was about to take an even deeper turn. This moment would be the last time it ever looked this way. If only I had known.

We hopped in the car and made our way to the hospital where the surgery was scheduled. My husband changed into his gown and we sat in the presurgical room for what seemed like forever. My nerves were, once again, on edge. Joel was prepped and ready, but I wasn't ready at all. There is no worse feeling than knowing someone you love so much is about to go into surgery. I felt helpless. Joel felt nervous. When a nurse came to tell him that they were about to take him back, he looked at me with fear in his eyes. I will never forget that look. He was holding his cell phone in his hands. When our babysitter forwarded me some pictures of our son, Joel asked if he could see them. As he studied the pictures, his face lit up and he seemed more at ease. He pulled up a picture of our son, held it to his forehead, and said over and over again, "I love you, bubby."

The time finally arrived to whisk him away. I squeezed his hand, trying to reassure him everything would be okay. I then leaned over his bed, kissed him on the cheek, and said, "I love you. I will see you soon."

Little did I know that was the last time I would ever see my husband in the normal state he was in. Had I known, I would have held him longer. I would have taken him in my arms and had him wrap his arms around me. I would have taken a picture of his smile, staying as long as I could in that moment of my husband as whole as he would ever be again. But we don't ever know the future, do we?

ↄ⌒

Six hours later I was sitting in the ICU by my husband's side. The surgery was successful, and he was still in ICU recovering. I'd walked in, surprised at seeing him on a ventilator. I had specifically asked before his surgery if he would come out on a vent, wanting to mentally prepare myself if that were the case. They had told us no, he wouldn't be. Walking in his room and seeing my husband was indeed on a ventilator upset me greatly. Finally the surgeon came in to see me. His eyes were large.

"The cancer was big," he said flatly. "Much, much bigger than what I had anticipated."

"Define big," was my response.

He held up his hands in a round motion. "I would say at least the size of a grapefruit."

No wonder Joel couldn't breathe. In that moment I felt waves of relief at the thought we had made the right decision. He went on to explain to me Joel would remain on the vent through the night to give his body a chance to relax. He said he should be off the vent by the time I got there the next morning. I had learned through prior surgeries you do not get any rest when you are sleeping on a hospital waiting room floor. As much as I wanted to be with my husband, it was almost time for them to kick me out because visiting hours were over. I decided to go home to try to get a few hours of sleep and head back over in the morning.

❦

I got there early the next morning and walked into Joel's room. He was still sedated and still on the vent. Again, I was not expecting this. It had been twenty-four hours since I had spoken with my husband. I was getting antsy and wanted him awake so I could talk to him and tell him everything was okay. He had told me before that he wanted me to tell him the results of his surgery as soon as I could. The nurse came in the room and said hello. It was my first time to meet her. She busied herself around the room, ending her visit with a vitals check.

"Hello, Joel, can you squeeze my hand with your right hand?" He squeezed.

"Good!" she said. "Can you wiggle your toes on your right side?" He wiggled his toes.

"Great. Can you squeeze my hand on your left side?" Her face scrunched up in an odd expression.

"Can you please squeeze on your left side, Joel?" Nothing. "What about your toes. Can you wiggle your toes on your left side?" Nothing.

I felt fear rising up in me.

"Um, nurse, what is going on? Should I be concerned?" I asked.

"I am going to page the doctor," she said and hurried out of the room.

Time went on and on. There was activity around his room, but a doctor had yet to appear. I was sitting in the chair as the minutes ticked away and seemed like hours. I could tell by the look on her face she was concerned, but I couldn't tell to what degree. All I knew was that I was extremely concerned myself and bracing for the reality that, once again, life might not be going as planned.

Finally, after an immense amount of time, the neurological doctor stormed into the room. He immediately walked to Joel's bedside and began screaming at him to follow commands. Not just talking, screaming. Joel was not responding. They kicked me out of the room, which filled quickly. There was activity and personnel everywhere. I was standing outside, all by myself since my family had yet to arrive, wondering what on earth was going on.

After a long while the doctor came over to me and said plainly, "Ma'am, we think your husband has had a stroke."

A stroke? What? He had just had surgery on his lung for cancer. Now the doctor was saying he thought Joel had suffered a stroke? He was only thirty-five. Did people that young have strokes? I was in shock and had no idea what this meant for us.

"I will have another doctor come talk to you but this

is very, very serious. We are taking him back to CT right now to get a picture of his brain. I will come talk to you when we have the results. Do you have someone who can come stay with you?"

When they ask you things like that, you know it's really, really bad.

Another doctor came to talk to me after the scan was done, telling me my husband had suffered a massive ischemic stroke and that the odds were very likely he wouldn't live. If he did, he would most likely become a vegetable.

My head was spinning. How on earth did we get here? We came in for a surgery for cancer. Cancer was our biggest obstacle, and now we had this stroke lumped on top of it? *Why God, why? Haven't we been through enough?* I couldn't make sense of it in my head, and neither could I imagine a reality where my husband did not exist. The rip current was back and pulling me deeper and deeper to a depth I feared I might never return from.

Doctors came into the room and gave me my options. I could consent to a surgery to remove a portion of his skull to allow his brain to swell. In doing so he would have only a one-in-four shot at making it through. My other option was to do nothing and allow his brain to swell to the point of no return, a certain death. Both choices were bad, both feeling like a betrayal.

I wept as I picked up the pen and signed my name on the dotted line, giving them permission to saw off a portion of my husband's skull. They hurried back to prepare the operating room. I turned and walked over to my husband. He still had the tube down his throat and his eyes closed.

"Joel, can you hear me?" I asked. "If you can hear me, squeeze my hand." He squeezed it.

"Good. Joel, listen to me. You have had a massive stroke. Doctors are saying it doesn't look good. They are about to take you back to have another surgery, this time on your head, to help with the effects of your stroke. Do you follow me?" He squeezed my hand.

"Joel, *do not* quit on me. Do you hear me? You keep fighting. I need you. Milo needs you. We *cannot* live this life without you!"

I was practically shouting as the tears were pouring down my face.

"God is going to be with you, and He is going to heal you. You just continue to let Him do His part, but you have to do your part. You have got to fight. You have to, Joel. You *do not* give up. We love you, JoJo. Milo needs his daddy. You have to be there as he is growing up, Joel. He needs you. I love you."

Each sentence was coming out in wild, erratic gasps. I didn't know in that moment if I was pushing my husband forward in his fight or if I was telling him good-bye. Over and over again he squeezed my hand, giving me signs he understood. With each squeeze, I knew he was vowing to fight with every bit of strength he had in him.

I stood there saying the same things on a repeat loop, for almost an hour, willing him to live and praying to God to spare his life. They finally came to get him to take him to surgery.

I squeezed his hand one more time and leaned down to whisper in his ear: "Joel, I love you. Do not leave me."

They wheeled my husband away for his second major surgery in less than twenty-four hours. Friends and family came to surround me as I sat on the dirty floor of a lonely hospital and wept.

∽

Against all odds, Joel made it through his surgery. He had a ten-inch scar wrapping around the right side of his head in a large U shape to allow his brain to swell. I sat at his bedside day after day, checking to make sure he was improving, whispering in his ear to continue fighting, massaging his feet with oils, and praying. They kept him mostly sedated because he had the ventilator down his throat and it was too uncomfortable to be awake. They would pull him out of sedation briefly each morning to do a vitals check and immediately put him back under. I tried to never miss when this would happen so I could look in his eyes and reassure him everything was going to be okay before he drifted off into a nice sedated sleep.

Finally, after four long days of sedation, it was time to remove the tube. It was a glorious moment. Only a few days prior I didn't know if I would ever talk to him again, and now I was able to hear his voice.

One of the first phrases he spoke was, "I love you, baby."

Since he was now able to talk, I knew the time had arrived to have the conversation I had been dreading. As far as I knew, Joel only thought he had gone in for his lung surgery. He most likely felt as if only a day had passed, and he was just now waking up from his sleep. The reality was nearly a full week had passed, and he would not be waking up to the body that he had presurgery. He was completely paralyzed on his left side. While it wasn't totally impossible for him to regain his strength, it would take a lot of work, and even then it was highly unlikely.

I braced myself and said a silent prayer for strength.

"Joel, I need to have kind of a hard conversation with you, honey," I started in.

"Is it about my stroke?" he asked.

"Um. . .you know about that?" I said hesitantly.

"Well, when I was on the vent some nurses came in to roll me over. They thought I was asleep, but I wasn't. I heard them say I had a stroke, I'm missing a chunk of my skull, and my left side isn't working. But I'm okay, baby, really I am," he stated simply.

I don't know if I was grateful he had heard the news that way or angry. Either way, he knew the truth, what lay ahead, and the hard part that was just beginning.

Now that the tubes were out, physical therapy could begin. This was one of the hardest parts of the process but necessary. He had no function whatsoever on the left side of his body. That meant any task he could only do with one arm. He wasn't able to walk, roll over, or sit up on his own. The stroke had also severely damaged the vision out of his left eye, making it nearly impossible for him to see unless he closed that eye completely.

He had been hit hard. It was heartbreaking to watch. I wasn't used to seeing my big, strong husband fully dependent on others to do the simplest tasks. But his fighting spirit hadn't gone anywhere. He was determined not only to rise but to astound.

Joel quickly made friends with the physical therapy staff and would crack jokes with them every time they came in his room. His attitude was amazing. Physical therapy was difficult, but never once did I hear him complain about how hard it was or even complain about the situation he was in. He continued to plow forward, working hard at his exercises and putting others around him at ease.

One time he had a particularly hard day and was easily worn out, so they told him that he should stop.

"No," he said. "Again." He was adamant.

"Are you sure?" the therapist asked. "You seem tired. . . you've done a lot today."

"I can do it. I want to do it," he said.

He told me later, "The more I push myself, the quicker I can get home. That is all I want, to be home with you and Milo."

They didn't know before, but the medical staff was realizing more and more what a fighter they had on their hands.

❧

The next night, we were finally able to bring Milo to see his daddy. I had been hesitant about this moment taking place because I didn't want Milo to be frightened by all the tubes. We put Milo in his stroller and slowly pushed him into the room. Joel's face lit up.

"Hi, buddy!" he said, "Come here, buddy!"

He looked over at Milo and lovingly grabbed his hand.

"Oh, bubba, I missed you so much. Daddy loves you, bubba. Daddy loves you."

Milo was antsy in my arms, wanting to be down on the bed with his daddy. I gingerly placed him at Joel's working side. As much as Joel wanted to hold him, he just couldn't. He only had one arm that worked and hadn't quite figured out the new way of doing things. Milo was frustrated, too. He didn't understand why Daddy couldn't roughhouse and play with him the way he always did. He didn't understand why he wasn't allowed to play with all the fun wires and tubes. Even though it was good for them to see each other, and good for our family to be together, it just wasn't the same. I left Joel's hospital room that day wondering if things would ever be the same for my little family again.

∾

Joel spent a few more days in the ICU and a few days after that on the floor. We spent Father's Day in a hospital room. Not ever the Father's Day that I envisioned, but at this point he was alive and that was what I had hoped and prayed for.

When the day finally arrived for him to be transferred to a rehabilitation facility, I felt like the largest of the bullets had been dodged. He was the one in four that had actually survived the stroke and subsequent surgery. People at the hospital were calling him a miracle man, and he was. We even got clear margins back from his pathology. We knew rehab would be hard, but it was the final step in getting him home to us once again. He was a fighter, and I knew he would fight hard to regain the use of his left side.

After two long weeks in the hospital, the time had

finally come for us to bid the staff farewell. The medical transport came to pick him up and take him to one of the best rehab hospitals in the state. Joel was beyond excited to be leaving. I will never forget the huge smile on his face and the conversations he had with the transport team. They noticed the thick East Coast accent immediately. He told them the story about how he married an Oklahoma girl and how I brought him back this way. He said he was nervous at first, but he loved it here. There was nowhere else he wanted to live. He loved the niceness of the people, and the laid-back lifestyle fit in perfectly with his laid-back attitude. He also mentioned it was a great place for a family, and he was so happy that his son would be raised here.

Once they got him loaded on a stretcher, they began to take him down to the waiting vehicle.

"Is it a limo?" he asked. "Because that is the only way I travel."

The transport team roared with laughter, and Joel smiled, thoroughly proud of his joke. I shook my head and rolled my eyes at his goofiness but stood in complete awe of his amazing attitude and fighting spirit. Yes, my husband might have changed physically, but the man I loved and adored was definitely still in there. Things were looking up.

CHAPTER 4
The Long Good-Bye

I swerved in and out of traffic, trying desperately not to lose sight of the ambulance in front of me. We had just left the hospital and were headed to the rehab facility Joel would call home for the next thirty days. The driver wasn't exactly driving as if he had a nervous wife tailing him trying not to get lost. I wasn't only lost in direction but in thought. How did we get to this place? My husband should be going home with me today—not to another facility where he would spend an entire month away from his family. As hard as it was for me, I know it had to be doubly hard on him.

Finally we arrived. I carefully unloaded the giant suitcase that held all of his clothes for the duration of his stay. I had packed all his favorite T-shirts, gym shorts, tennis shoes, and sweatshirts to make sure he was comfortable; after weeks of hospital gowns, I imagined real clothing would feel like a treat. I was sure to bring his favorite pillow from home, his beloved sleep machine, and his favorite blanket. I also brought loads of family pictures and taped them to his wall. I knew it would be hard moving from one hospital to another, so I wanted to do what I could to make it feel homey.

As I wheeled the huge suitcase to his room, I thought about how long this entire journey had seemed and braced myself for at least another thirty days at the rehab center. I tried to keep it in perspective by realizing we were on the downhill slide and the worst part was behind us.

I rounded the corner to his bedroom to find him lying in bed already looking spent. At rehab there were no IVs and no wires or tubes connected to him. He looked the most like himself he had in weeks. It was a welcome sign.

I started to busy myself unloading all of his clothing and hanging the pictures on his wall.

"When do you think they are coming for me?" he asked.

"What do you mean coming for you?" I replied.

"You know, to start my therapy," he responded.

"Oh sweetie, you won't have any therapy this afternoon. The only goal for today is to get you here and unpacked, settled, and rested so you can be ready to start up bright and early tomorrow."

"But I want to start today," he insisted.

"It's nearly five o'clock. All the therapists are heading home for the evening. Trust me, you need to rest as much as you can for tonight and get ready to go at it tomorrow," I reasoned with him.

"I just know that the quicker I get this done the quicker I can go home. So I really wanted to start today. But I guess I can wait one more day." As soon as the words left his mouth, he let out a big yawn and quickly drifted off to sleep.

The rest that day was much needed. Rehab is no joke. He had therapy four hours every day, both physical and occupational. He had to learn how to do everything all over again. He had to find techniques to help him transfer from his bed to the wheelchair, to get from his wheelchair to the toilet, and his most favorite job, how to walk again holding the bars. He liked that one the best because it felt as if he was doing the most work. He also had to relearn how to do the small things, like brushing his teeth, washing his face, and getting dressed all with one arm—all the things we take for granted on a daily basis.

It was hard to watch him push himself over and over, even harder to watch him so physically impaired. Through it all I never once heard him complain. The only time I would ever see him down was when he would talk about how much he missed home and our son.

You can have special moments in the hospital, and I almost let one pass me by. It was on a day after work when I came to see him. A nurse had just taken him to the bathroom and was transferring him to his bed. This process alone could take up to a half hour, exhausting him every time. For some reason she was insistent after she got him in bed that I "crawl in bed with him." When she first said it, I thought it was funny. Hospital beds aren't exactly known for having room for two. If I was ever in Joel's bed, it was to sit at the end. She was insistent, so I asked Joel if he wanted me to lie down with him. He surprised me by saying yes.

It wasn't easy to maneuver myself in a way that was comfortable for us both, being that his left side was paralyzed. Still, I found a way to wedge myself beside him on his right side. I laid my head on his chest, and he wrapped his arm around me and rubbed his fingers through my hair, kissing my forehead softly. I closed my eyes and pretended we were at home in bed relaxing together and watching TV like we used to do. It was the closest I had physically felt to my husband in a very long time. We continued to lie like that in silence for a long while. I finally tilted my head up to see that his eyes were closed, too, taking in the moment just as I had been. I tenderly kissed his cheek.

"I love you so, so much, Joel, and I am so proud of you," I said through quiet tears.

"I love you, babe, and I'm proud of you, too. You're doing a great job. I know it's not easy," he said.

"Don't be proud of me. I'm not the hero. You're the hero, and you're our hero," I told him.

I looked up at him to see a big smile on his face that didn't disappear as he faded off to sleep.

⁂

Joel was working hard at rehab but not progressing very quickly. He was encountering a lot of pain from the two surgeries he had endured. Much of the day they had him medicated to combat it. The pain was getting worse the more exercises he would do, so as time went on, we had some loopy conversations.

One day, however, we had a conversation that would change my life, for the rest of my life.

Joel's back was hurting, and he asked me to help him sit up in bed so I could rub it. I quickly obliged, glad to give him relief in any way I could. We both sat quietly as I rubbed light strokes, in a circular motion. Finally, he broke the silence.

"Babe, you and I are going to have another baby. It's going to be a girl."

I was taken aback, first by the fact he was talking about children at such a time. We both remembered our infertility problems and how difficult it was for us to get pregnant. We currently had two embryos in storage, but in his current condition, I didn't see any way we would be able to try to use them to have another child.

"Okay...," I said nonchalantly, hoping he would drop the subject.

"No!" he said boldly. "You are not listening to me. We are going to have another baby, and it's going to be a little girl. You know what you're supposed to name her."

I remembered the baby girl name I had in a dream years prior. A name I had never heard before. When I woke up from the dream, I looked up the meaning and was shocked it was the exact meaning of Joel's name: "Jehovah is God." I told Joel the name, and we both liked it and decided if we ever had a girl, that would be her name.

"Ellis?" I asked.

"Yes, Ellis. That will be her name," he replied.

Just then he started to yawn, and I gingerly put him back to bed. *What a random conversation that was*, I thought, as I put it away in my mind for safekeeping.

❧

The next day was my son's first birthday party. Sadly, we were not at home celebrating as we had planned. Instead, we had booked a conference room and would celebrate at the rehab center. Nothing fancy, just some cupcakes, presents, and enjoying the day as a family. Joel was not happy about any of this. He felt awful that his illness was causing us to have to celebrate our son's first birthday in the hospital. We had tons of conversations about it, and he finally listened when I said the most important thing was he was there celebrating with us. We promised each other no tears that day, and even though it wasn't the celebration we wanted, we were still going to celebrate. It was a hard day, but we made it through. After an hour-long celebration, I wheeled Joel back to his room, and the nurse helped me to get him to bed. She asked him if he enjoyed the party. Joel smiled big and said he had. I knew better. I gave him huge hugs and told him good-bye for the evening. After walking out the door, I paused outside, peering through the crack.

It was then, when he thought everyone had left, in the silence of his room, that he started to cry. I rushed back in beside his bed and held him close.

"JoJo...," I started in, unsure of how to finish.

"I know, baby, I know I promised no tears. I'm sorry. I just miss the little guy so much. I miss him and you. I want to come home. I want to be home now," he said, tears pouring down his face.

"Babe, you know there is nothing we want more than to have you home with us. Nothing. And you are so close. You just need to keep fighting hard to get strong so that you can be home with us," I said.

"I'm trying, I'm trying so hard," he said, still crying.

"I know you are. You are fighting hard, and we are so proud of you. Milo and I love you. We want you home with us and we know you will be, but you've got to get a little bit stronger. You are so close, honey," I said.

"I will keep fighting. I'm fighting hard every day. Do you believe me?" he asked.

"Of course I do," I said without hesitation.

That was the problem. I knew he was giving every ounce of himself, and we were still so far from tangible results. He didn't say it, but I know he knew it, too. The deadline for his release was coming soon, and he was still so very far from where he needed to be. It scared me. I didn't know what the future held for him or for our family. The unknown was terrifying.

I stayed for a while longer and held his hand until the tears stopped and he was ready for sleep. I walked over to close his blinds and turn on his sleep machine, and I pulled his blankets over him. I kissed his forehead like I did every night before I left.

"I love you, Joel. I will see you tomorrow," I said.

"Love you, too, babe. Good night."

Little did I know that was the last time I would ever hear those words from my husband again.

I got to the rehab center a little later than normal the next day. Since I had been gone so much the past four weeks, I wanted to spend some quality time with my son that morning. When I arrived at the center, Joel was asleep.

I sat in the chair beside his bed and read a magazine, patiently waiting for him to awake.

He finally did an hour later. In seconds it was clear. Something was wrong—very wrong. My gut told me to get him help and get it now.

I ran down the hall to the nurses' station. "Something is very wrong with my husband. I think he has had another stroke. If someone is not here in the next few minutes to give him a scan, I am going to take him out of this hospital bed and carry him to the ER. Something has to be done *now!*"

I meant it, too. Joel weighed about 185 pounds at that time. I have no idea how I would have managed to carry him out of that room, but I was desperate and would have put him on my back and crawled on the linoleum floor to the ER if I had to.

The nurse on duty looked in my eyes and knew I was serious. Fifteen minutes later they came to take him to CT. Just a few minutes after they had brought him back and put him in his bed, the doctor came back in the room. From the moment I saw his face and body language, I knew. My suspicions were correct.

"He has an immense amount of bleeding in the brain. We have to take him to the hospital now. I am calling the transport team."

Bleeding in the brain. Another stroke. How on earth

could he have had another stroke? We had just gotten past the first stroke, and he was in rehab. I didn't understand how we were back to having another stroke.

I didn't have time to burst into tears. The ambulance would be here in a few minutes. I ran around the room, throwing all of Joel's things into suitcases. The pictures I had hung on the wall to remind Joel of home, in hopes he would be home soon, were hastily ripped off the wall. The nurses were working on him, and the room was complete chaos. The transport team showed up soon and loaded Joel onto a stretcher. I grabbed his hand, telling him I loved him and we had to go back to the hospital to check some things out.

No response.

By the time we got there, our family and friends were starting to show up. The look on everyone's faces scared me. I was inconsolably weeping and shaking with fear. I could not believe we were back at the hospital.

They finally let me back to be with him in the ER, explaining he would be waiting there until a spot opened back up in the ICU. By this time they had put Joel back on a ventilator and had him sedated. My dad was back there with me. We sat in silence. A doctor finally entered the room.

"I just saw his CT scan. And it's bad; it's really bad," she said.

She was telling me what I already knew. Then she took

a deep breath and started in. "You know Joel has been through a lot, and he has fought very hard. Sometimes the most compassionate thing you can do is to think about the person's wishes and what he would want. Would he want to live the kind of life he is going to live?"

I could not believe what she was insinuating. She was trying to tell me, in that moment, the best thing to do would be to decline care for my husband and let him die. I was furious.

"Actually, Doctor, I know *exactly* what my husband's wishes are. We talked about it at length and have advance directives. He wanted every avenue exhausted in trying to save his life. He has a family and a young son. He told me to never give up on him, and I never will. So I need you to do every single thing that you can to save my husband's life and nothing less." I looked her square in the eye as I said that.

"Okay. . . ," she said hesitantly. "But I need you to know this is very bad, and you are going to have some very difficult decisions in front of you. But we will do what we can." She turned and quickly exited the room.

They did try. For an additional two weeks, Joel was in the ICU on a ventilator. They hooked him up to a machine to cool his body in an effort to reduce swelling to his brain. I was by his bedside every day. After he got off the vent the first time we were in the hospital, he had told me he had heard the things we had said to him. Knowing this made it all the more important for me to talk to him now. I explained to him all that had happened. I willed him to keep fighting. I told him how much I adored him.

Finally, it appeared the time had arrived when they could begin to unsedate him and remove him from the vent. He was getting better, and I was thrilled I would hear his voice again and hug him tightly. My dad came to spend time with him in the hospital that evening so I could go home to tuck my son into bed. I left feeling a sense of calm and grateful anticipation for what the next day would bring.

I was home for less than an hour when my phone rang.

"Sarah, it's Dad. Um…they are going to take Joel back to CT right now," he quickly said.

That didn't make any sense. He wasn't scheduled until the morning. Why would they be rushing him in right at that very moment when he was scheduled for the next day? Something wasn't right. I didn't get a chance to spit out all my questions before a member of the neurological team took the phone from my dad.

"Sarah, when they went to check on Joel, his eyes were fixed and dilated and not responsive. We are taking him to CT. This is not good at all. You need to come back to the hospital now."

Just like that, my world crumbled once again beneath me. We were so close, a day away, in fact, from good news. Joel was doing well, and the doctors had been the most optimistic with me they had ever been.

Why now? God, why is this happening? I thought.

I quickly kissed my son good-bye and raced the entire thirty-minute drive back to the hospital, praying not to get pulled over. As I drove, I was so distraught I was dry heaving, wracked with sobs.

I finally got to the hospital and walked back to his room. It was a teeny-tiny room; there were no fewer than ten people inside. My dad was standing outside the door, white as a ghost.

"Something went very wrong," he told me. "I don't know everything that happened, but they had *a lot* of people in there working on Joel."

I peered in the room and caught the eye of the woman I had spoken to on the phone. She came out to talk to me.

"He nearly coded on the way to CT. His breathing tube came out, and we were seconds away from having to shock him," she said. "I've seen the scan, Sarah, and this is bad. You just need to know it's really, really bad."

They later confirmed it was another third and massive stroke. Once again, I felt like I had been kicked in the gut. When would this ever end? Would we ever catch a break? We were so close. So close.

Before I left for the night, I walked over to her, and she gave me a hug. She kept telling me over and over again how sorry she was. I could tell by the look in her eyes she thought it was over. I was not willing to concede. We had fought too long and too hard for Joel to lose this battle now.

"I just believe that somehow, some way we are going to still get our miracle," I told her.

She looked to the ground, then to Joel, and then to me.

"I hope you do, Sarah. I really hope you do."

Even as she said it and meant it, I knew wholeheartedly she didn't believe we would ever get it.

⁓

It was the morning after, and the hospital routine was the same, but things definitely felt different. As I sat in the giant chair beside Joel's bed, my legs to my chest and a blanket around my shoulders, the doctor entered the room and sat in the chair beside me. Neither of us said a word as we both stared intently at Joel.

"I had a hard time sleeping last night. This one hit me hard," he started off.

"I didn't, either," I said softly, still looking at Joel.

"I told you that I would tell you when there's no hope," he said and then paused. "There's no hope."

The words I had been praying I would never hear were just uttered. They hung in the air, heavy with meaning.

Unable to feel any lower than I had ever felt through our journey, I asked softly, "What's next?"

"The only option is for us to declare him brain dead. Then we have to legally turn off all forms of life support. I can do the first part of the check today, but we will have to wait another forty-eight hours or so to do the last part of the check. If he fails both of them, then that will be noted as his time of death and the machines will be turned off when you are ready."

"Okay," I said.

"Is there anything else I can answer for you?" he asked.

"No," I simply said.

"I'm really sorry. Truly I am."

I nodded silently in agreement, staring straight ahead.

I knew he was, but not for the same reasons that I was. We were two people in the same situation but two very different realities of what that situation meant for us. He was losing a patient; I was losing a husband. I couldn't wrap my mind around what had just happened. I wanted to scream but also dissolve in tears. I asked God over and over again how I would make it through the horrifying reality of what was ahead of me. I knew He promised to always be with me, yet in this moment, He had never seemed so far away.

They came back a little while later to do the first part of the brain death test. I held my breath and closed my eyes. I couldn't stand to watch. I once again prayed, pleading with God for a miracle. When I heard the doctor taking his gloves off, I knew the test was complete. I raised my head to look at him. He shook his head.

"No signs of brain activity. We will do the last part of the check once his levels get to where they need to be so the test is uncompromised and complete."

And with that the doctor left.

⁓

It wasn't forty-eight hours later—it was actually seventy-two. Seventy-two hours I cried out to God and prayed like never before. I knew how things looked and knew it did not look good. I also knew God had been with us the entire time and performed many miracles on Joel's behalf already. I didn't believe He would stop now. Not even a little part of me did. When fear would grab hold at the thought of attending a funeral or being a single parent, I would stop those thoughts right in their tracks.

"My husband will live and not die" was a mantra I repeated out loud over and over again. "My husband will live and not die."

The morning finally arrived when his levels got to where they needed to be for the final part of the check. Part of me was relieved we would finally have resolution; part of me was dreading to know what that resolution would be.

The morning drive to the hospital was so beautiful: a perfect sunny, unusually mild summer day. I parked my car, walked to the building, and hit the button to the second floor, repeating the same routine I had done daily for nearly two months. My parents and three close girlfriends met me there. The nurses did not waste any time in calling in the doctor to perform the test. This was a new doctor, whom I had met only once. He entered the room, nodding professionally.

I sat down in the big chair beside Joel's bed, just as I had many days before. As he explained the details of the test, I crossed my legs and bent over, curling into a ball, hiding my face. My girlfriends surrounded me on every side, rubbing my back and holding my hand. My parents were in the corner beside us. During this check they would physically turn off the breathing machine several times in a row to see if Joel would start to breathe on his own. They would also put water in his ear and other annoyances to see if he would respond. The small room was jammed with respiratory techs, nurses, and the doctor himself. It felt as if all the walls were closing in on me.

"We will go ahead and begin the test now," the doctor said.

I heard him mechanically going from one part of the test to the next. Over and over again I shut my eyes and willed my husband to breathe. Even the smallest of a breath would signal that there was still reason to hope.

Breathe, Joel, breathe, I would say again in my mind. *Come on, please, please breathe. God, please.*

The test continued for several minutes until I finally heard the doctor ask for the time.

That is when I knew. Joel had failed the test, and this was his time of death: 9:36 a.m., Friday, July 23, 2013.

The hospital staff gave their condolences and told me we could have some time with Joel before the machine was turned off. Our friends and family used that time to pray over Joel and sing his favorite songs to him.

By 11:00 a.m. the time had come to turn off the machine. The nurses and respiratory personnel came in and removed the tubes and machines within minutes. As they quickly exited the room, I sat by Joel's side and held his hand. I knew the time was drawing near. Still, for a long while, I begged God to let him live. I begged God for a miracle. I begged Joel not to leave. I knew it was against all odds, but I was determined to keep my promise to Joel and fight for him until the very end.

About ten minutes later, I felt a tangible shift in the room. I knew my husband's spirit, the essence of who he was and not the shell of his physical body, had left the room. My heart was broken.

It was over.

I nuzzled my cheek to his cheek, buried my face deep

within his shoulder, and cried. Everyone left the room to give me a moment with my precious husband, the love of my life, the man present for me every moment of the last nine years. I'd waited a lifetime for Joel to enter my world, and now our planned life together had been stolen from us. It felt unfathomable to have found my life's greatest love and know the rest of my life would be spent apart from him.

I looked at him lying in that bed and realized in an instant I had not only lost my best friend, but my son had lost his father. I also knew at only one year of age my son would never remember him. That thought brought an aching pain to my innermost being.

How do you say good-bye to someone you love so much? I didn't know.

I sat beside his bed, gently taking his hand and placing it on my head, as if to comfort me as I wept. The loss was deep, the pain so heavy, I could hardly breathe. My greatest fear had come to life. After several moments I stood, went over to my bag and grabbed the oils I had used to soothingly rub his feet every day of his hospital stay. I poured the oils into my hands and rubbed his feet one last time. Upon finishing, I walked over to his side and whispered in his ear: "JoJo, I know you know how deeply I loved you. You fought so hard, and I am so very proud of you. Milo is proud of you. Not one day will go by that our hearts will not ache for you. I love you. I love you.

I love you. Good-bye, my one true love."

I gently placed his hand I held back onto the bed and kissed his cheek once more. I went to grab my purse and belongings and walk out the door. Before I left, I slowly turned around one last time to look at him, knowing my eyes would never again see the man who I loved more than my own life. I wished it was my own life that left instead of his, or at least with his. I couldn't imagine living life without him.

I walked out of the ICU in a trance, not believing the finality of what had just occurred. My three dear friends were waiting in the hall ready to enfold me in their arms. I cried, telling them I couldn't believe this had happened. I wanted so badly for Joel to get his miracle, and I always believed he would. I cried for my son, who at this moment was oblivious to the fact he had lost so much. I cried for our hopes and dreams, which had taken years to build, only to be gone in an instant. I cried for the pain I felt then and the pain I had yet to endure. I cried for the life my husband would never get to live and the life he had to endure at the end. I cried for the memories we had and the memories we would never be allowed to have. I wasn't just grieving losing a person; I was grieving the loss of our entire life.

Gone in the blink of an eye.

My girlfriends looped their arms through mine,

steering me to the elevator and down to the parking garage. As we were about to step out the door, I hesitated. I had come in through this same door earlier that morning and I still had a husband. I was still a wife. No longer. I now exited the door having just lost my husband, myself a widow. It was unreal the difference a few hours could make, a life here at one minute and gone in another. Nothing about it made sense to me.

"In these doors with one life, and I now walk out with another," I told my girlfriends. "When I leave this hospital, I don't know what I am walking into. I just know that life will never be the same." Tears were pouring down my face.

They looked at me and nodded slowly with tears in their eyes. There was nothing they could say.

With that, I took a deep breath and slowly but surely walked out the door.

CHAPTER 5
The Decision

I opened my eyes, turning to my left, to the empty spot in my bed. It took a while for my brain to catch up to what happened the day before: my husband was never coming home. Suddenly, a bed that once seemed at times crowded was all too large. Silent tears poured down. It felt as if they would never stop.

Today was the day I would go to a funeral home and plan my husband's service. The thought was overwhelming. Writing his obituary the night before was heartbreaking enough.

The day ended up being as difficult as I'd imagined. Every choice at the funeral home was, well, old. From the programs, to the flowers, it all reeked of stiffness. Of course it was geared toward their main clientele, which was not men in their midthirties. No one that age should die in the prime of his life. My family, girlfriends, and I worked hard to pick out choices that were youthful and vibrant and spoke to who Joel truly was. We used a Valentine's Day print I had made Joel that year, with twenty of his best characteristics, as the program guide. We planned a balloon release, scheduled for after the service, and planned to play songs he loved. We tried with everything we had to plan a personal service that spoke to the spirit of who he was. It was an exhausting and emotional process.

I was spent when I got home from the funeral home. My mom took my son into the playroom so I could have some moments to myself. I was in my closet changing into comfortable clothes when I looked over to a picture of Joel and me on top of my dresser—a photo-booth style. The first photo we were smiling normal, the second I was kissing his cheek, and the last we were sticking out our tongues to the camera. I stopped and stared at that photo, having the sudden realization that as I continued to age, I would one day look back at that photo and see my younger self with my husband, who would never age another day. Something about that thought brought me to hysterics.

I started sobbing violently, and before I knew it I was on the floor wailing, curled up in a ball. I was screaming out over and over, "I can't live without you, Joel. I can't do it without you." The tears were flowing so fast and freely that the carpet beneath me was soaked, as was my shirt, from sweat and tears.

In the middle of my sobs, I had a picture in my mind of Joel standing over my curled-up body and holding me. It was so real and vivid. He had his entire body over mine and was cradling me. My outstretched hand was held in the palm of his, and he was stroking my hair. He was quieting me, telling me it would be all right and he would always be with me. Realistically I knew I was imagining it, but it was so vivid and seemed so real, as if he were really there. It was as if I could feel his very real presence right beside me.

I don't know why my mind was creating this vision, but I never wanted it to stop.

After several moments the tears slowed, and I started to quiet as I felt a sense of peace wash over me. In my vision I saw Joel start to get up and tiptoe away as if he were thinking, *She's better now, I am going to quietly leave the room.* I started to go into panic mode. Now I was crying even harder and screaming, "No, Joel, no. You can't go. Please don't leave me again. Please don't go. Please, Joel, stay with me. You can't leave me. Please."

No matter how many times I asked, he still left. This time I knew it was for good. Cold emptiness washed over me once again. I stayed on that floor weeping from the most primal place within me in ways I had never wept before and hoped to never weep again.

❧

The morning of Joel's funeral, I woke up to a thunderstorm raging outside. The rain echoed how I felt in my heart: dark, gloomy, and angry. I got up and dressed in my funeral day best. Shopping for my dress had been a nightmare as I wandered aimlessly around the store muttering to myself, "Joel, which dress do I pick?" Even the smallest of decisions seemed monumental to me.

As I finished applying my waterproof mascara, I heard someone say the limo had arrived to take us to the service. I didn't want to have to face what I was to face that day, yet I knew I had no other choice. It was time to honor my husband.

We pulled up to the church, and I stayed in the limo until it was time for them to seat our family. As my dear friend Julie sang "Great Is Thy Faithfulness," the funeral director held my hand and asked me if I was ready.

Everything within me wanted to yell, "No! No, I am not ready! Please don't make me go in there."

I didn't. Instead I said a silent prayer for God to somehow give me strength.

As I walked into the room, everyone looked up. I felt the discomfort of hundreds of eyes peering at me in my weakest moment. I silently looked at the floor. They sat us in the front row, and I looked at the massive family pictures spread across the front of the church. Photos we had taken during our most happy times, now on easels commemorating Joel's death. It was unbelievable to me. I wanted to speak to honor him but knew there was no way I would be able to do so without breaking down into a sobbing mess. Instead, I wrote a letter and had our pastor read it.

> *I wanted to speak so badly on behalf of my husband*
> *but did not believe I could get through it, so I come*
> *to you with this letter. Our family has so much*
> *overwhelming gratitude to everyone that has*
> *prayed and interceded for us over the last three*
> *years and especially the last seven weeks. We thank*
> *all of you. We especially want to thank our Antioch*
> *church community, who have embraced our story*
> *and believed so completely for Joel's healing. Your*
> *prayers will not return void. Joel and I always felt so*
> *humbled to be able to be a part of such an incredible*
> *community of people.*
>
> *How do I even begin to describe how amazing*
> *this man was? Words cannot do him justice, but I*
> *will try my best. Everyone who knew Joel would*
> *come to him for everything. If your computer would*
> *break down, Joel would be the person people would*
> *call, and he would walk them through how to fix it.*
> *If he knew you were going to buy an item, electronic*
> *items in particular, watch out! He would scour*
> *newspaper ads and the Internet to find you the best*
> *deal possible. People thought his passion about it was*
> *so silly, but really it was his way of always taking*
> *care of those around him that he loved so much. If you*

were in his life, he loved you deeply.

I will miss the laughter that filled our home even in the midst of extremely difficult circumstances. I remember when he was going through chemo the first time, we were watching TV and he casually said, "Babe, do you mind if I buy some Godzilla slippers?"

I responded by saying "Uh. . .that should be fine," rolling my eyes, and that was the end of it.

I had forgotten about that conversation until about two weeks later a huge package arrived at our house. Joel opened it, and out came a pair of insanely huge Godzilla slippers, with claws and everything. He wore those ridiculous slippers all winter long. Sometimes we would be in the midst of a serious conversation and I would look down at his feet and burst out laughing. He was so childlike at heart, and it was one of the things I loved the most about him.

He loved God. His faith wasn't one where he shouted it from the rooftops but rather quietly tried to display the Lord to people every single day. One of my favorite recent memories of him happened just two months ago. After the May 20 tornado, his heart was devastated. He wanted so badly to do something but couldn't help with cleanup due to how sick he was. He came up with an idea to load up our car full of water and drive around giving water to people cleaning up the rubble of their homes. Block by block I would drive around, and he would roll down the window yelling out to people, "You guys need any WATTA?" in that glorious New York accent of his. He had the biggest smile on his face that day and said he was so glad he could do something to help those people. His heart was always full of compassion for those in need.

His love for his son was beyond compare. Our son was a miracle we had prayed for—for five years. Sometimes we would be in the living room watching Milo toddle around, and I would look over at Joel and he would have tears of joy rolling down his face. He would always tell me, "I just love that little guy so, so much." Our promise to you, Joel, is that your son will know every single day how much his daddy loved him. He will know who you were and will be raised to be every bit of the man that his father was.

When Joel was in the hospital, he told me he felt like God would one day put him on a stage so that he could tell everyone about how good God was and how if He had healed Joel He could heal them, too. He said, "If they see me hopefully I could just give them hope." Sweet Joel, God did put you on a stage for the world to see you fight, and fight you did. And we know that your desire for others to see Christ's hope in your life will not ever go unfulfilled.

Many people have felt for me as a wife [for] having to go through such a difficult three-year health battle with my husband, but I want to say it was truly the greatest honor of my life. Through our suffering we got to know God in ways that many people never get to experience. We got to see with our own eyes the way He would provide for us and move in miraculous ways. We got to experience three years of a deeply intense bond with God and with each other because there was no one else who could understand more intimately what we were walking through. Life was sweet and each day appreciated so fully because we were never under any assumptions of how long our time together would be. When we said "in sickness and in health," neither of us could have imagined what that would entail, but I would walk this road a thousand times over again with Joel and with the Lord leading us. My greatest sadness will only be that we didn't have more time together. No amount of time with the love of my life would have ever been enough.

I want Joel's life to not be in vain. I want his story to touch millions and for nations to be changed by the story of this man. Through every trial he never complained. He always told me it would be okay and

God would take care of him, and He did. We grieve because we will miss him every day until we see him again, but it is hard to be sad for Joel when we know that he is with the Lord in the most amazing place and with our child that we lost. I know half of our family is there waiting for us and will rejoice with us again one day. That hope carries us. Until then, precious Joel, Milo and I will carry you so deeply in our hearts and honor you with our lives. We will continue to proclaim your story until all will see and truly know "how great is our God."

We love you.

To end the service, our pastor had us all stand and cheer for Joel as loud as we could in order to tell him, "Job well done." As I heard the cheers echoing, I placed my hand to my heart and whispered to him softly, "This is all for you, JoJo. It's all for you."

&

After the service we gathered thirty-six balloons in honor of his thirty-sixth birthday, which was three weeks away. Friends and family congregated outside as we stood in a circle to bow our heads in remembrance of the life of the most amazing man.

All of the nine birthdays we spent together rushed through my head—from the very first one in the awkward beginning stages of dating, to the very last one we celebrated with our newborn baby boy. Life had been so good to bring us together and so cruel to take him away. I shut my eyes and told him I loved him. He would never be forgotten. I knew where he was now—celebrating the best birthday he had ever had. Then I looked up and released the balloon into the Oklahoma sky. I watched as the wind carried all thirty-six of them away.

❧

Later on that evening I sat around the dinner table with my husband's four best friends. We had made it through the highly difficult memorial service and were now having a memorial service of our own. This one involved food, stories of my husband, and much-needed laughter. Looking around the table was bittersweet. How wonderful it was to have those who knew my husband the best with me in that moment. How horrible it was to not have him there with us. His absence was heavy.

I knew this would be my only chance to have them all in one space to ask them the question that had been burning in my heart since the very moment my husband passed away. For even the day he took his last breath on this earth a piece of him was still here, albeit in a not-so-conventional form. Two tiny little embryos left over from our first IVF cycle were in storage mere miles from my home—a piece of my husband and a piece of me. After losing Joel, it was all I could think about. What was I going to do with those embryos? The thought that it was even possible to have another pregnancy after his death was both terrifying and exhilarating. I knew what my heart was telling me, but I needed confirmation. I needed to hear from those who knew him best. I needed to see the looks on their faces as I shared the possibilities. I needed to know where they stood. As difficult a day as it was, I knew it had to happen now. There would be no other opportunity to do it in person.

The last few years of our marriage had been filled with a battle, a battle for my husband's life. Now that the fighting was over, I felt like a weary warrior who had fought with all I had, only to lose the war. Yet, beyond the pain of loss there was something on the horizon. Hope from the depths. Hope that though my husband was no longer here, a piece of him had yet to grace this world with its presence, bringing life and joy to what was so cruelly stolen. Hope that the sun would feel as if it were breaking through the clouds again. Hope that what we fought for would never be in vain. Hope that out of the ashes a beauty was rising again. Hope that from the deepest depths was coming a melody, a new song from our lips, a song of triumph.

"Guys, I have a question I need to ask you."

I looked down at the table and fidgeted. Suddenly,

I was at a loss for words and unsure how to begin. I stared at my fingernails, then the table, and then the wall. Hesitant.

The guys were getting impatient with my hesitancy. One of them finally broke the silence and spoke up.

"Sarah, whatever you have to say, spit it out. Just go ahead and say it."

There was no more time to wait. The script I had rehearsed previously in my head had now gone out the window. I had nothing eloquent, just my heart to share.

I took a deep breath and let it out.

"Okay," I started in slowly. "So I have these embryos. . . ." My voice trailed off. They looked at me blankly, clearly not sure what I was getting at.

"Do you remember how Joel and I got pregnant with Milo using IVF?" I asked.

"Of course we do," one of the guys responded.

"Well, we have two embryos left over. An embryo is the start of a baby, and it is what they would put inside my body for me to possibly get pregnant."

I looked around the table at each of them as the realization of what I was telling them started to take root. Confused faces immediately turned to grins.

One of them spoke up first. "Sarah, you know you *have* to have this baby, right?"

Instant relief. No judgment from them whatsoever.

"Oh my gosh," spoke up another, slowly shaking his head. "That is incredible. Incredible."

"So what are you asking us?" a third asked me.

"Well, you know, it's just kind of odd. Joel is gone, yet I still have the ability to have his baby. It's weird and awesome all at the same time. I don't know what people will think of me. I didn't know what you guys would think of me."

"Who cares what *anyone* thinks! You know this is exactly what Joel would want you to do, right?" one of them asked.

"Of course I do. We talked about it. But talking about it and going through with it are two completely different things," I answered.

"Well, don't worry about us. You have our support one hundred percent. It's what he would want, it's what we want for you, and we just pray it works," he answered.

I slowly looked around the table at the excited and supportive smiles of the men who knew my husband best. Their support meant the world to me. I didn't have to decide then, but I would soon. Knowing how they felt made the decision much easier to make. I could arrive at my conclusion later. For now I wanted to relish the moment with these men, laughing until we cried and missing the fifth New Yorker who should've been at that very table with us.

As the weeks passed, the tight circle of support surrounding me started to loosen as people understandably returned to life as normal. The problem was there was no life as normal for me anymore. My entire life as I knew it died when my husband did. I spent a considerable amount of time in a fog and a state of shock and disbelief at what had occurred. My day vacillated between precious moments with Milo that brought a smile to my face to fits of crying and despair. It hurt so badly, and as the days wore on, it got worse, the emptiness leaving me feeling even emptier. In my extreme state of stress and grief, I started to develop hives all over my body and would spend many hours curled up in a ball on the floor trying to keep myself from scratching them, only to break out worse when I did. I looked it up on the Internet to see what on earth was happening.

Your body has no more tears to cry, it stated, so the hives are another way to release the pain. Not having tears to cry wasn't a problem for me. They flowed from me in endless streams. The pain, it seemed, would never end.

One week later it was my birthday. I told my friends and family I didn't want to celebrate that day, wanting it to be as any other. It was unfathomable to even think about celebrating a year of my life without Joel there.

Later on that afternoon, I received a phone call from the funeral home telling me my husband's ashes were ready to be picked up. Of all days, the call came on my birthday. It made an already miserable day even worse.

I made it through by pretending it was just another day—until that evening. I was putting a document in a seldom-used drawer beside my bed when I saw a stack of old cards and letters Joel gave me I had thankfully saved. I pulled out the stack and grabbed every single birthday card I had from him. I decided this was how I would celebrate my birthday—with my husband. I spread out the cards on my bed and read them one by one. I cried as I saw Joel's familiar scroll, allowing myself to remember the memories attached to each birthday in particular. I let myself stay in that place long enough until I felt myself teetering too close to the edge where I knew a sobbing fit was imminent. I started to gather each card together and put them back in a pile.

Before I slipped them into my bedside table, I took one last peek at the last birthday card Joel ever gave me.

"Love you so much. Can't wait to spend the next thirty years together. Hope you had a great day; you deserve it. Love you, my best friend."

I could barely contain myself at the thought I would never again receive another birthday card from him.

I would give everything I possessed for just one more anything from my very best friend.

ᐯᐯᐩ

Two weeks later was another difficult day, Joel's birthday. We tried mightily to make the day special, celebrate the day of the one we loved, without him there beside us.

My idea for his birthday this year involved the outdoors. I headed to the backyard with my son, kneeling in the grass with Milo to keep him from taking off. We were about to head into the house, eat our cupcake, and sing "Happy Birthday" to my husband. Before we did, there was one last thing we had to do. Though I chose for my birthday not to be celebrated that year, Joel's would be every year. We would honor him every day in our home and in our hearts, but August 14 would always be a day of cake and celebratory stories of the life of a man who left us far sooner than he ever should have. Just like on the day of his funeral, I purchased a small batch of birthday balloons in bright colors and different shapes. I tried to wrap my hand tightly around the balloons while keeping the other arm around my son.

"Now, Milo, these birthday balloons are for Daddy in heaven. We are going to send them up to him now to tell him happy birthday and that we love him."

My son looked at me and smiled, replying back in pure baby gibberish. How thankful I was for this baby boy, the most glorious piece of my husband I still had left on this earth. In that moment, I wasn't completely healed from my grief—not even close. I still didn't know what was in store for my son and me. All I knew was that somehow, some way we would move forward and would always tell the story of a man whose legacy was one of love, wholehearted faith, and extreme perseverance. We may have had to say good-bye prematurely, but we knew we would see him again. He would never be forgotten, always loved deeply by those of us who knew his heart and his beautiful soul.

I looked toward the sky and ever so softly said the words, "It's all for you, JoJo. All for you. Oh, how I love you."

With that I held my son close to my side as we released our birthday balloons into a gorgeous, vast, bright blue Oklahoma sky.

❧

Summer faded into fall and fall into winter. Months had passed with one of the most important decisions I'd ever have to make hanging over my head. I'd weighed the pros and the cons. I had thought it all through until I was sick of thinking it over anymore; there was no turning back, my decision was made.

My hand shook as I picked up the phone and dialed the familiar number. A receptionist answered the phone.

"Hello, fertility clinic," she said.

"Yes, this is Sarah Rodriguez. I would like to set up an appointment to do a round of IVF, please."

PART II

THE RISE

CHAPTER 6
A Love Story Continues

I tapped my finger on the steering wheel, waiting impatiently for the light to turn green. I was cutting it close in making it on time to my appointment. This wasn't just any appointment; this was *the* appointment.

Red turned to green not a moment too soon. Two quick right turns and I was now in the all-too-familiar hospital parking garage. My mind started to fill with memories from the last time I was there. It was my six-week checkup after my son was born, my husband still alive. We were reeling from a cancer reoccurrence while also basking in the glow of a brand-new baby boy. It was a trying time but one I would give anything to go back to.

I put my gear in PARK and hopped out of the car, walking briskly through the double doors. As I walked, my mind was in overdrive. Many months were spent in preparation for this moment. Would I be able to walk this journey alone? Would it work? What if it didn't work? What if it did?

With my hand trembling and stomach churning, I scribbled my name on the sign-in sheet. In my mind I was already rehearsing what I was going to tell the doctor. No matter how many times I had gone over my prepared statements, I was wracked with nerves. Besides my friends and family, this was the first person outside of my cocoon to know my plans. I had a small circle of my nearest and dearest who loved me who knew of my decision and supported it fully. I had no idea how anyone else would respond. I felt as if I was letting others into a deeply vulnerable space. The feeling was scary and uncomfortable.

I looked around the waiting room at all the couples, walking their pregnancy journey together. It felt unreal to be starting this journey alone. Looking at the door to the office, it still was as if Joel could walk right through, his presence instantly calming my fears. It wasn't to be. This time there would be no partner to walk alongside me. As much as I had prepared myself for the notion, the full weight of it was hitting me hard. I bit my lip and struggled to hold back the tears. Was I insane for what I was about to do? I momentarily considered walking out the door and changing my mind. Before I could make a run for it, the door flew open.

"Rodriguez, Sarah," the nurse called out loudly.

Her familiar voice snapped me out of my thoughts. There was no more time to debate, no more time to rehearse—the time was now.

They took me back, weighed me, and took my blood

pressure. Once they were done, I was led to an exam room, asked a few more questions, and told the doctor would be in soon. I sat on the examination table, waiting in silence. I looked around the room as again, the memories of my last pregnancy with Joel nearly brought the tears to the surface. Not one to show every emotion, I hadn't prepared myself for just how difficult this all would be. Deep breaths in, deep breaths out.

Finally, there was a brisk knock at the door, and the doctor entered, followed by a nurse. He was wearing a smile, totally unaware of the bomb I was about to drop on him.

"How have you been?" he asked.

I paced myself, not wanting to spill my guts within the first ten seconds.

"I have been well," I replied.

"You ready to go for this again?" he asked.

"As ready as I'll ever be," I answered.

I lay down on the table while he did a physical examination of me, charting and measuring everything he needed for the IVF procedure. Once he was done, he grabbed my hand and helped me to my upright position. The time had come to share my heart.

"Doctor, I have some news to tell you." I hesitated then went in with full force. "Not long after my son was born, we received the news my husband's cancer had returned. He fought it for a full year before he passed away this last summer. I will be going through this IVF process without him."

As I spoke, the tears I had been trying so hard to hold back began to run down my face. The look on both their faces was total shock as the nurse silently grabbed tissues and placed them in my hands.

No one said a word.

He finally broke the silence. "So you have two embryos left. We are putting them both in, and you are wanting them to work?"

"Yes," I responded. "I have thought long and hard about this. I have prayed about it, and I feel like we should put them in and the rest will be in God's hands."

As I spoke, the tears continued to flow. I tried in vain to make them stop. They wouldn't. The last thing I wanted was for my doctor to think I was an emotional basket case. Truly, I wasn't. There had been so many emotions leading to this decision. The fact that I was saying my truth out loud had brought a tidal wave of feelings to the surface. Yes, many of them were sad, but the majority of them were excited anticipation for what was to come. Stepping off the ledge was the hardest part, and step off I did.

I could tell the doctor was feeling a little perplexed at the entire conversation, but he recovered well.

"Okay. We will do our best," he said.

With that, he left the room. Only the nurse and I remained. She unexpectedly rushed over to give me a huge hug.

"I am sorry for crying," I told her. "I'm okay, really I am. I just had a bit of a moment, but I promise, I will be fine."

She nodded and gave me one more tissue before leaving the room.

Alone, I breathed a sigh of relief. One of the hardest parts was over. I put on my clothes and exited the room, telling the nurses I would see them again soon. The next thirty days of the process would involve the doctor and the fertility clinic personnel. Only if I conceived would I return to the OB office.

Next, I headed over to the second part of my appointment—this one at the fertility clinic itself. There I sat in another, smaller lobby, filled with more couples. I was the only person in the room alone. It is a sensitive place to be, each person knowing the reason why you are there. The discomfort in the room is evident, especially with the husbands.

My name was called, and I headed back. They took my blood and additional information to begin. After that I was ushered to a small room to go over my medication for the following month. I looked at the printout schedule they gave me in order to keep the dizzying amount of medications straight. The nurse walked me through how to do the injections that would be a part of my life for the next month and additional three months, should I conceive. It wasn't as scary as the first time we did IVF. I knew what I was in for. Still, the sheer amount of work and scheduling involved was a bit overwhelming.

"Now that we're done going over your schedule, do you have any additional questions?" the nurse asked.

"No." I shook my head. "I don't think I do."

"Okay," she said. "It looks like I have all of your paperwork completed. I just need you to take this last page home, get your husband's signature, and return it to us."

I paused, not knowing quite what to say, and ended up blurting out the first thing that came to mind.

"Actually, my husband is deceased. I will be doing this cycle alone."

"Um, okay," she said, clearly startled. The room was deafeningly silent for a moment. "I am going to go check on something, and I will be right back."

She left swiftly, leaving me alone in the room, the awkwardness of the moment still lingering in the air.

A few minutes later, she returned, only this time she was not alone. A veteran nurse I knew from our last go-around accompanied her.

"Hi, Sarah," she said tentatively. "How are you?"

"Hello, good to see you," was my reply.

"So, the nurse told me about your husband. I am sorry to hear that," she started in.

"Thank you," I said softly, not sure what other words to ever use when I was given condolences.

"When you and your husband filled out your initial paperwork, do you know what box you happened to check on what would happen to the embryos if you were to divorce?"

"No," I answered, confused at the question.

"Well, the thing is, we have never had a situation like this before," she finished.

"Okay. . . ," I responded, still unsure as to where she was headed.

"We don't have a box that states what exactly should be done in a situation like this. We want to make sure we are handling it the right way, but it's a situation our lawyers may need to be involved in. The divorce box is as close as we can come to an answer as to your husband's wishes for the embryos if he is not in the picture."

I was momentarily stunned and then quickly infuriated at the implication. I might have a battle on my hands over my own flesh and blood? I racked my brain, trying to remember the conversation Joel and I had about the potential embryos. I remembered telling him it would be silly if we divorced for him to have the embryos. It was not like he could use them himself, and it's not as if a fictional wife number two would want to implant the ex-wife's embryos in her body. While we both laughed at the imagined scenarios we were asked to comb through, it was important issues we were considering. Although I remembered the weightiness of it, I did not remember the conclusion we arrived at.

"Well, I will tell you one thing," I said in a calm voice that belied how I was feeling inside. "If you, or some lawyer tries to tell me what to do with my own biological embryo, you are going to have one heck of a battle on your hands."

Instantly, I think, she could tell how insulting her words had been. She immediately backtracked.

"I'm not sure it will even come to that. If the doctor is fine with proceeding, and you checked the box saying the embryos would be yours, there shouldn't be a problem."

She was trying to make it better, but she had shown her hand. They were hesitant in my proceeding with the process. It had taken all the strength I had within me to walk through those doors and confidently tell them of my decision. I knew in my heart what I felt like I was to do, and I would go through with it despite what others thought of me. Now, here I was, being told I might have to fight for the ability to go through with what I had fought to be brave enough to endure.

There was nothing left to say. I was told they would have to pull our old records out of storage and I would receive a phone call in a few days.

Forty-eight hours later, my phone rang with a call from the clinic nurse. I felt breathless with anticipation as I answered with a frantic "Hello."

"Hi, Sarah, it's the nurse at the fertility clinic," she said cheerfully.

I held my breath, afraid of what would come next.

"I wanted to let you know we pulled your old records, and you both did mark the box saying the embryos would be in your possession. So, everything should be good to go for you to start on your IVF."

I exhaled deeply. The relief was instant. Nothing was standing in the way. I was really going to do this.

A huge smile lit up my face as I thanked her. She asked me to come by the office the next day to sign off on a form and we would be good to go. I hung up the phone and turned to look at my one-and-a-half-year-old son, who gave me one of his big, toothy grins. I wrapped him in my arms and gave him kisses all over his face, while the sound of his loud giggles filled the air.

Oh, how I hope this boy gets to be a big brother, I thought.

❧

The next day I was back at the fertility clinic to sign off on the final form I needed to proceed. The nurse pulled out my chart and began to flip through it. She landed on a page and showed me the old signatures she had referenced. There I saw my husband's large and loopy signature above mine. Seeing it in person brought back another wave of emotions as I tried mightily to swallow them down. She continued on to the back of the chart.

"I am going to need you to sign, riiiiiiiiiiight here," she said, directing me to the wife line while the husband line stood empty above.

I quickly signed my name on the line, just wanting to be done.

"I want you to know, we all think you are very brave," she told me earnestly.

Stunned, I didn't know quite what to say. She was one of the first oppositions I had encountered in my decision. Now, her opinion had softened.

"Thank you," I said. "That means a lot to me." I meant it. It did.

"I hope you get the results you are wanting," she said.

"As do I," I responded.

There was nothing more to say. The results were in God's hands. I was so thankful they were out of mine.

৵

The next thirty days were a normal cycle of IVF. I would take fertility drugs and shots daily. At a certain point, I went in every other day for ultrasounds and blood work, to see how everything was progressing. The nurses liked what they saw. Everything was rolling along as it should. The way things were lining up, I would have the embryos implanted a few days after Valentine's Day.

This was my first Valentine's Day without Joel. While it was never a largely important holiday to us, it still stung not having him there to celebrate. My girlfriends rallied around me, several sending flowers and chocolates and taking me out to dinner.

The day after, Milo and I went to breakfast with my friend Liz, who would accompany me to the implantation. As we were seated at our table she started in excitedly.

"Sooooooo, are you ready for this week?" she asked.

"As ready as I'll ever be," I said wryly.

"Are you nervous?" she asked.

"I'm not nervous about the actual procedure because I know what to expect. I am nervous about the results. It's been such a work up to get to this point, what if nothing happens?" I asked.

I explained to her the odds of normal IVF success, which were a little below 50 percent. The doctor had sought to quell my expectations by reminding me that IVF with frozen embryos had much lower odds, more around the 30 percent mark. I knew there was a small chance the embryos could not survive the unthawing process. I also knew I had a miscarriage with Milo's twin.

That was always at the back of my mind and another risk to contend with. As much as I felt a purpose for this child, there were still many fears to face.

"I don't know," she said. "I get what you're saying, but I just think it will happen. It just all seems meant to be, you know?"

"I hope so. I really do. It seems hard to even imagine being pregnant and doing this on my own," I admitted.

"Well, you're not ever alone. I'm here, your friends are here, and your family is here. Don't ever feel alone," she said sincerely.

I knew what she meant. As thankful as I was for her encouragement, I also knew the end result, good or bad, would be one that would have emotional ramifications all my own.

"You're so sweet, girl," I told her.

"I'm just so excited to be with you. I know you would rather it be Joel, but I'm honored it gets to be me. I just still can't believe it. Your life is kind of crazy," she said.

"Crazy doesn't even begin to describe my life most days," I said with a hearty laugh.

We finished up our breakfast and headed out the door with a week of unknown expectation waiting to greet us.

❧

I woke up four days later, quickly hopping out of bed and heading to the shower. Implantation day had finally arrived. Liz and my mom would arrive in an hour to take me to the hospital. My thoughts had raced all night long as nerves kept me awake. I stood in front of the hot water, willing it to wake me up and calm my worries. I couldn't believe the day had finally arrived. All the tears, the prayers, the fears, the wonder, had all brought me to this moment in time. I didn't know what was ahead, but I knew I had done all I could do. The outcome was up to the Lord.

I finished my shower and dressed in comfy clothes. I pulled my hair in a messy bun and threw a protein bar in my bag for a snack on the go. Forty-eight hours of bed rest was to follow, so I made sure my sheets were fresh and I had a pile of reading material stacked high. I tidied up my room and house, knowing it would be the last time I would be able to do so for a few days.

Just then, my doorbell rang, signaling the arrival of one superexcited Mom and an equally excited Liz.

Liz handed me cards from several of my girlfriends, one to open each hour. Each card was filled with encouragement, scripture, and reassurance of prayers. I smiled as I opened the first one and tried to hold back the tears. Milo came running around the corner, and I enveloped him in a huge good-bye hug.

We stopped for a quick lunch on the way to the clinic so I would have a full belly during the implantation.

Though I largely stayed quiet, nervous energy abounded as we talked over food. It was incredible the amount of thoughts that were racing through my head.

Today was the day. Today, though my husband had died, a living piece of him was going to be placed inside my body. It was almost beyond comprehension. I wondered what was in store for my life if this were to work. I wondered what was in store for my life if it didn't. It felt as if I was standing at a fork in the road and today would be the start of one direction or the other. No matter what was to happen, I was relieved we would soon reach a long-awaited conclusion.

We arrived early and made our way to the stairs to the second floor. By this time the entire staff knew of my story and seemed even more excited than we were. They took us back to the preop room and put me in the very same bed I was the first time. I looked at the chair in the corner, where my husband once sat. Closing my eyes, I pictured him in his scrubs, a huge grin on his face, while waiting to enter the procedure with me. Looking at the chair, now empty, brought a tinge of sadness to my heart.

They listed the familiar instructions: going to the restroom one last time, and undressing from the waist down, wrapping a blanket around my body. The nurse handed my mom her scrubs since she would be taking Joel's place today. Once we were all changed and ready to go, we sat on the bed waiting for them to come.

An embryologist came in the room to confirm my name and the fact that I had two embryos left and would be implanting them both. I had chosen to do two, just as I had my first IVF round, to increase the chances it would work. My doctor always said, "We implant two with the hope for one." While I could never only root for one embryo to work, I was fine with one or both taking. The woman had me sign off on the procedure one last time.

"I just wanted to let you know that your embryos look really, really good. They are still the same grade and look exactly as they did when we first froze them. That is unusual. Typically they change and degrade a bit upon freezing," she stated.

"So that's a good thing?" I asked.

"Oh yes. That's a very good thing," she said with a smile.

As soon as she spoke the words, instant calm washed over me. I remembered the talk Joel and I had while he was in rehab. He had told me we would have another child. He was emphatic about it. That was one of the driving forces leading me to my decision. This was the first part of the day, and we were off to a positive start already. I knew the Lord was with me, but in that moment it felt as if Joel was, too.

❧

The time came for them to take me back for the implantation. I read the very last card my friends had given me, once again touched by their thoughtfulness. Liz gave me a huge hug and a thumbs-up sign. I held the blanket tightly around my waist as my scrub-clad mother and I made our way back to the room.

It was just as I remembered, sterile with bright lights overhead. They had me lie on a bed with my legs in stirrups, much like it was during a monthly exam, only this time it was awkwardly in a room filled with people.

The doctor made his arrival and greeted us warmly. He asked if I was ready to go, and I nodded in response. He looked at my mom, then to me with a smile.

"All right," he said. "Let's get started."

The room was silent as he began the procedure. When he asked for the embryos, I knew the time had arrived. I said a silent prayer to the Lord, asking for success, but surrendering to His will at the same time. My heart filled with joy at the thought of a part of Joel about to become a part of me. A quick tear of thankfulness slipped down my cheek, thankfulness I was even able to be doing what I was doing. Fear left, and hope abounded.

I clutched my womb and spoke directly to the embryos.

You are both loved, and you are both wanted, I said in my mind over and over.

It was the same mantra I had repeated during my first IVF round. I believed in the power of prayer and positive thinking. I tried to imagine those embryos going inside my body and burying themselves in, just as they are supposed to. I imagined positive pregnancy tests and holding a baby in my arms. I imagined the joy I would feel at successful results.

You are both loved, and you are both wanted, I repeated again.

"Okay," the doctor announced. "We are all done," he said as he pulled the blanket down over me. "You are pregnant until proven otherwise."

With that, he patted my arm and left the room. My mom looked at me with a huge smile as the nurse came to transfer me to a rolling bed. From there they took me back to the preop room, tilting me at an angle, a position I would assume for the next hour.

When that was done, they put me in a wheelchair to escort me to the car.

As they pushed me out past the nurses' station, the ladies gathered round.

"Good luck, Sarah!" they said.

"We will see you back here in ten days," one said.

"Ten days?" I asked, surprised. After my last cycle, we had results in seven days. Waiting an additional three days to see if your life was about to massively change seemed like an eternity.

"Yes," she said with a knowing frown, "it is ten days now. But don't worry, it will be here before you know it."

She patted me on the back as another came over to give me a quick hug.

It felt good to be done. The worst part of the drugs was over. My only job now was to rest and do one additional daily shot. That I could handle. It had been a long road, but we were finally reaching the finish line.

I lay down flat in the backseat of the car for the ride home. As I tried to rest, I could hear my mom and Liz chatting up front while Journey's "Don't Stop Believing" played over the radio. I laughed at the silliness of the situation.

I never knew what it was like to get pregnant in a "normal" way. My normal included doctors, nurses, drugs, shots, procedures, and surgeries. Now, after that was all said and done, I was lying in the back of a car wondering if I had just gotten pregnant. It was a sensation that was odd the first time and even odder the second.

Touching my belly, I marveled at the life that could be inside. Oh how badly I wanted this to work.

You are both loved, and you are both wanted, I spoke again to those teeny-tiny embryos now hopefully making my body their home.

We arrived home, and my mom gingerly helped me out of the car and to my bed. I hugged Liz good-bye, thanking her for her support on such an emotional day.

Bed rest was not something I enjoyed. It was hard for me to sit still for days at a time. Being a single mom, I never had two days to myself in bed. I had no idea what I would do to occupy the time. Only two hours in, and I was going stir crazy.

Milo finally awoke from his nap and crawled into bed with me to spend some time watching movies. He, of course, had no idea what Mommy had been up to that day. No idea why I tried to keep my rambunctious boy from jumping on my bed and crashing into my belly. No idea how life was possibly about to change.

As we lay on that bed, I finally got him to settle down. He cuddled close to me, and I ran my fingers through his dark, curly hair, leaning in to take in his smell. My boy. Half his daddy in biology and 100 percent his daddy in spirit. He walked like him, talked like him, stood like him, laughed like him, looked like him. He had been a constant source of strength for me in this year of grief. I was determined to never let him see me cry and to only know his mommy as strength and peace. He, in turn, brought unlimited amounts of joy and laughter to our home. Many days I would wrap my arms around him and close my eyes, savoring the moment. All his daddy had ever wanted was to see his boy grow. It was his biggest fear he would not be able to.

"Sometimes when I'm rocking Milo to sleep, I tell him how much I love him, and to not worry, Daddy's not going anywhere," Joel once told me.

Knowing how deeply he wanted to be here, only not to be, made me try to take in the moments with my son all the more. And in this very moment, I was taking it all in and then some. I held my son close, whispering a prayer once again to the Lord.

"Please, please, please let this work," I begged.

CHAPTER 7
Life after Death

I walked into the local CVS, keeping my eyes peeled for anyone who might know me. The last thing I wanted was to bump into someone during this covert operation. Of course the item I needed was at the very back of the store. It would not be an easy in and out. As I walked toward the pharmacy section, my eyes checked each aisle to ensure I would not bump into a familiar face. In Oklahoma, running into someone you know is not a hard thing to do.

Time is a funny thing. It goes by far too quickly when you are willing it to slow down. When you want it to speed up, it mocks you by stretching into endless hours and minutes. I had to wait ten days. Ten days to find out the results of a possibly life-changing procedure. After the allotted time had passed, I was supposed to go back to the clinic for a blood pregnancy test. Then I would find out results after an hour. They warned you not to take a home pregnancy test because it was so early you might obtain a false negative, only further heightening your stress and worry.

During my first IVF, I followed instructions just as I was supposed to. This time, I was finding it a little harder to obey. Each day I would will myself to just wait, repeating their warnings that the test could be negative and I would worry unnecessarily. Then again, it could be positive. . . .

This was to be the last time in my life I would ever have the chance to be pregnant. Never before had I found out I was pregnant the normal way, by peeing on a stick. I had done so in the past only to receive bad news. If there was ever a time to break the rules, it was now. Since I would never again have the opportunity to find out if I was pregnant, I decided to do it on my own terms, not in a hospital setting. That is how I ended up finding myself at CVS on my drive home from work.

I quickly reached the back of the store where the pregnancy tests are kept, still hyperaware of my surroundings. Only a select few knew of my pregnancy intentions. The last thing I needed was for someone I knew to run into the widow buying a pregnancy test a mere six months after losing her husband. Talk about an easy way to get the rumor mill started.

I reached for the box that held two tests inside, just to be sure. Also, for good measure, I picked up a giant bag of peanut butter cups to buy along with my tests—both to make my first purchase less awkward and to have on hand in case I needed to drown my sorrows.

Thankfully I was able to make my purchases and get back to my car without any interference. I stuffed the bag in my giant purse and made my way home.

Later that evening my parents came over to visit with Milo and me. When everyone was playing and not paying attention I slipped out of the living room, heading to my bathroom. I closed and locked the door, making my way to my purse, where the pregnancy test was hidden. Carefully, I opened the box, reading the instructions several times to make sure I did everything correctly. Basic instructions—pee on a stick, wait three minutes, rejoice or cry, in that order. I followed it to a T, and soon I had a pregnancy test sitting on my bathroom counter, as I assumed my position from years past, sitting cross-legged on the floor.

One, two, three, four, five, six, I counted slowly in my head until I reached sixty, three times in a row.

It was time. My legs were shaking and my heart beating fast as I stood to my feet. I reached forward to look at the test.

Positive!

For the first time in my life, I saw a positive pregnancy test. Tears filled my eyes. Could it be true? It had worked! I was going to have a baby. Our baby. It was one of the most joyous moments of my life.

I sat there for a moment and thanked the Lord. Then I looked to the ceiling.

"We are going to have a baby, Joel," I said with a grin.

The moment seemed special and all our own, for in that moment, we were the only ones who knew the news. It wouldn't stay quiet for long.

I left the bathroom, test in hand, and headed to the living room, where my parents were with my son. Without saying a word, I handed the test to my mom. She looked at me in shock. Then I handed it to my dad.

"Well, you knew this was going to happen, didn't you? Joel told you that you would have another child!"

I was still in disbelief. I knew what Joel had told me but had remained cautious in my belief it could actually be true. After years of trying to get pregnant, begging to be pregnant, I had tried IVF twice and twice had been successful.

Reaching down to Milo's level, I pulled him in close.

"You are going to be a big brother, bubs," I said softly.

He looked up at me and smiled, having not a clue what that meant.

I put the test on a table and took a picture, eventually sending it to the three girls in my life who knew what was happening. I received a flurry of excited responses.

Though we had all expected it, we were all still shocked it had actually come true.

Later that night I lay in bed with my hand on my belly. Pregnant. I had trusted my gut, gone out on a limb, and it had worked. Wow, it had worked. My heart was bursting with thankfulness. I knew it wouldn't be easy to have another child on my own. This was never the path I thought my life would take, but that was true in many instances. All I knew is this baby was loved and wanted and had a deep purpose for its life. How else can you explain the incredible way it came to be?

❧

The next morning I took the second pregnancy test, for good measure. It, too, was positive, this time the plus sign showing up even more clearly. At this point I had no doubt; this was really happening. It wasn't all just in my head. God was blessing us with another child. It was a gift of life, from the giver of life—a gift I had wanted so desperately and now accepted so humbly.

I still had to go in for my ten-day pregnancy test at the clinic, and I wasn't looking forward to telling them I hadn't listened to their warnings. Since the results were positive I hoped they wouldn't be too upset at me.

They called me back to the room where my blood would be drawn. The nurse wasted no time in asking the big question.

"So, did you cheat and take the home pregnancy test?" she asked with a smile.

The way she worded the question made me believe I wasn't the first and certainly wouldn't be the last. I let her question linger for a bit before I replied.

"You know, I didn't do it my first time with IVF, but ten days is a *really* long time to wait. . . ." I left her hanging.

"Aaaaaaand the test said?" she said anxiously.

"The test said I am having a baby," I responded.

A huge smile erupted on her face.

"Yay, yay! We tell patients a negative pregnancy test can be incorrect, but a positive one won't lie. You really are pregnant."

Word traveled fast in that little clinic. By the time I had used the restroom, gathered my belongings, and was heading out the door, I had a small crowd of staff gathered around.

"Oh my goodness, Sarah, you had a positive test!"

"We can't believe it," another said.

"We are so happy for you," said yet another.

"Are you just beyond belief excited?"

I was excited but also overwhelmed at their exuberance. I smiled in return, thanking each of them for their well wishes.

The last encounter was with the veteran nurse, who

stood quietly, right beside the door. As I moved forward to make my exit, she stopped to give me a hug.

"Congratulations. You are one brave woman," she said as she wrapped me in her arms.

I didn't feel brave, and didn't need to, only blessed.

Forty-five minutes later the phone rang, and I received confirmation my blood test had shown I was indeed pregnant. An ultrasound would be performed two weeks later to find out if it was one or two babies. Until then I would go about life as normal, trying to pretend it was, when at that moment life was anything but. The clouds had rolled back. Light was peeking through. Our family was growing.

❧

It didn't take long for two weeks to pass. My body had finally begun to show signs of a pregnancy with morning sickness turning into all-day sickness. I was tired and exhausted already, chasing around a toddler and trying to keep my symptoms at bay. The day finally arrived to return to my OB's office for an ultrasound. My friend Lauren accompanied me so I wouldn't have to brave the appointment alone. It was nice to not have to sit in that waiting room all by myself. I was so grateful for her company.

They called my name and walked me back to the ultrasound room, instructing me to change my clothing and lie on the table. It wasn't long before the doctor arrived.

"Well, hello there," he said as he entered the room.

"Hi," I said with a smile. "Me again."

"Yes, it is," he replied.

I could tell he was tempering any form of happiness for me until he was able to perform the ultrasound. He was, as he always was, trying to quell expectations until a confirmation could take place.

"Let's see what we've got going on in there," he said as the nurse flipped off the lights in the room.

He started in, moving around the wand. I looked to my right to the giant TV screen that showed exactly what was happening. There, I saw the most beautiful sight to behold. A small flicker of light.

Boom, boom, boom.

A heartbeat. Life. A teeny-tiny baby. Half-Sarah, half-Joel. No, he was not here physically, but his DNA was in full glory on that television screen.

The doctor continued to look around my womb.

"It looks like there is only one in there this time," he concluded.

When you have two embryos being placed in your body, you want to root for them both, or at least I did. Both lives were loved and wanted. In my abnormal situation, I had continually placed the results in the Lord's hands. He knew exactly what I could or could not handle. Having a toddler, along with twins, as a single mother would have been a lot. I trusted in His purposes. The disappointment did not linger long. One baby was meant to be, and one baby was what I would have.

"Only one, huh?" I asked.

"Yes, just one," he confirmed. "But the heartbeat looks great, and the baby is measuring perfectly."

He reached over to push a button on the machine that allowed me to actually hear the baby's strong and beating heart. Whooshing, full, strong, steady.

I looked over at Lauren.

"Wow," she said. "Unbelievable."

The doctor printed off pictures from the event. You could already see the baby's tiny little arms and legs. All pregnancies seem like a miracle, but this one was beyond a miracle. Everyone in that room knew it, and everyone quietly stood in awe.

He wrapped up the procedure and told me to call if anything abnormal happened. I jumped off the table, got dressed, and clutched the picture of the tiny, perfect little human growing inside my very womb. Life had visited me once again, and I willed it to stay.

The weeks wore on, and thankfully, nothing abnormal occurred. I sailed through my first trimester with flying colors, breathing a huge sigh of relief to reach the end.

My pregnancy was progressing normally, just as it should. Miscarriage fears flew out the window, and with each passing month, it became all the more real; I was having a baby.

At the end of my first trimester, I decided to tell the world my news. By the world, I mean my little world. I started to show much faster this time and couldn't keep the secret much longer. Eleven weeks in and my pants no longer fit as my belly grew fuller and rounder by the day. I decided to break the news the way most news is broken these days—via social media on my blog. The reaction was swift and all very positive. I had been worried about the opinions and judgments of others, unnecessarily. If anyone disagreed with my decision, that person was not voicing it to my face. It was fine with me if it remained that way. The secret was out; I would have to hide it no longer.

Eighteen weeks in my little baby had grown enough that a gender could be determined. I excitedly called to make the appointment. There was something about finding out the gender of the baby that made it even more real. The baby went from being called an "it" to a "he" or a "she," a "son" or a "daughter."

The morning of the ultrasound I awoke and dressed quickly. I put on my favorite necklace, a thumbprint of my son and a thumbprint of my husband, that I wore constantly. It felt good to have a piece of my husband present, constantly around my neck for me to remember he was still close in my heart. I walked to the kitchen and poured the first of many glasses of water I was told to drink in order to obtain a clear picture. My mom and I kissed Milo good-bye, left him with the sitter, and hopped in the car to head to the appointment.

Upon arrival, we were greeted by my friend Lauren and also my sister, Annie, each bursting with excitement.

"What's the verdict?" asked Lauren. "What do you think it's going to be?"

"Well, if Joel was right, I know it's going to be a little girl," I responded.

"Do you have a gut feeling?" asked my mom. "Do you really think it will be a girl?"

"I don't know. Lately, I have been feeling like maybe it *could* be a boy," I said, not wanting to commit either way.

All I wanted was for them to be able to determine the gender that day. I had heard horror stories from excited friends going in for the gender reveal, only to be told the little dear had his or her legs firmly crossed. They were then told to wait a few weeks and return. There had been so much buildup to that day already, I couldn't imagine waiting any longer. Patience was never my strong point.

The couple before us left the room. Ultrasound pictures

in hand, they walked out shaking their heads.

"The baby sure was being stubborn, wasn't she?" asked the dad.

"Thank goodness you were finally able to get her to put on a show," the mom said.

As they passed us, she stopped to wish us good luck and uncrossed baby legs. The time had come for us to make our way back to the room. I was beside myself with anticipation.

The tech had me lie down on the table and quickly got to work. She moved the paddle around, and looked, and looked, and looked. She crinkled up her nose and made a face.

"It looks like this baby is going to make me work for it, too," she said.

"Oooooh no," I started in. "Please, please, try your best. I am dying to know."

"I know you are," she answered. "Don't worry, I am an expert with stubborn babies."

She continued to move the paddle around, pushing different sides of my belly to jostle the baby into submission. Each time, my beloved child would move for an instant and then return to a little ball and go back to sleep.

It was beginning to look like it wasn't going to happen when suddenly the baby moved and the tech let out a low whistle.

"I think I saw what it is," she said happily. "Give me just a few more minutes, and I am going to see if I can get a little clearer shot."

My heart started to beat fast. I looked over to my cheering squad, who had their faces scrunched in anticipation, trying to decipher what they were seeing on the screen.

"Yup," she said finally. "I saw what I needed to see. Congratulations, Mama, you are having a girl."

The tears started to flow. My mind raced back to that day at the rehab center a year prior.

"Babe, you and I are going to have another baby. It's going to be a girl."

Joel had told me. I wanted to believe him then, but I didn't see any way his prediction could be true. He had been through too much; we had been through too much. Yet here I was seeing his very words lived out. God had given us a promise, and my husband was audacious enough to speak it out. Now I was seeing with my very own eyes, his belief turning to truth.

I clutched my necklace, tracing along the lines of my husband's thumbprint, wishing more than anything he was here in this moment.

"You were right, JoJo. A little girl. You were right," I said softly.

I looked over to the group, who were hugging and

crying, and laughing and cheering.

"Don't cry," the tech said, seeing my tears. "You will make me cry."

"I'm sorry," I responded. "I just knew it was going to be a girl. I knew it."

"Really?" she asked. "Well, how did you know?"

My reason was marvelous, and miraculous, powerful, and true. But in that time and space, I didn't want to offer an explanation of all the whys and hows. In that moment I just wanted to marvel at my husband, and the goodness of the Lord. His promises were true, and my husband was the first to know it.

"Oh, just a feeling," I said with a coy smile.

A few weeks later was one of the harder moments in our family amid the joy of our coming little girl. It was the day that would've been my ninth wedding anniversary. My eighth wedding anniversary was spent with Joel in rehab. My parents had put together an anniversary dinner and brought it to the center. I had a nurse help me put Joel in a wheelchair and roll him down to the conference room to celebrate. The spread of food, roses, and candles was impressive. Still, it was less-than-ideal circumstances to say the least. Never in a million years could I have imagined that would be our last anniversary and meal together. Or that the next anniversary would be marked by being pregnant with his child yet without him.

Life had thrown many curveballs, but I would choose to rise. Despite how I felt inside, I would spend the day thinking of the man of my dreams and honoring our love. My girlfriends put together a dinner at a local upscale Italian restaurant. Ten of my favorite ladies gathered around the table to celebrate Joel and me. The talk quickly turned to giggles and chattiness, as most girl time together does.

"Tell me about how Joel proposed to you," one of them said.

"It was really sweet but low-key. I was always worried he would do it in a public place like a basketball game. So I made him promise it would be just us. In the end he did it at his apartment. He handed me a dozen red, white, and yellow roses. He told me the yellow roses symbolized friendship, the white marriage and forever, and the red love. He said, 'Sarah, I promise to love you and be your best friend forever. Will you marry me?'"

The table erupted in claps and a chorus of awwwww-wwws.

"Great job, Joel!" said one of my girlfriends.

The conversation then turned to my wedding day and how some people wait for their wedding day for their first kiss.

"Did you do that?" someone asked teasingly.

"Um, no," I said to them laughingly. "I am *way* too much of a planner to have not planned my wedding day kiss."

"Wait," another said, "let me get this straight—you planned your wedding kiss?"

"Of course I did! We had photographers there. I had to know the general direction of which way his head was going and where I should put my hands. It turned out just fine, and we enjoyed the practice," I said with a knowing smile.

Some couldn't contain their disbelief, and others admitted they, too, had practiced their wedding kisses. The laughter and stories continued for hours on end, with tales of my husband filling the space. The evening came to an end with hugs, sweet cards from my friends, and slices of Joel's favorite chocolate caramel cake. Friendship and laughter were just what I needed to get through a difficult anniversary. There was no one I wanted there more than Joel, but if he couldn't be, this was a close second. We only got eight anniversaries together. Only eight. Still to this day, it hardly seems fair. Our forever was a shorter lifetime than I had planned but packed full of the most love I could have ever hoped for. You pledge at the altar in sickness and in health, never knowing the full scope of what that could mean. Yet I would promise it all again, even knowing the ending that was to come. The depths of the pain would be something I would always live with, but so was the overwhelming gratitude of walking through it all with him by my side.

A mere three weeks later, another anniversary loomed, the one I had been dreading. July 23, 2014, the one-year anniversary of my husband's death. For months I had thought of this day, what it would look and feel like. I couldn't imagine any way I could get through it. A moment of inspiration hit me that changed everything. Joel's favorite thing in the world was acts of service to others. What if we all joined together and did random acts of kindness for others to honor his life? I mentioned it to several friends who loved the idea. I decided to title it the Choose Joy Project. In the midst of our sorrow, we would make a choice to choose joy over sadness and to honor him by blessing others. It was the perfect idea.

I posted the idea on social media, and to my surprise, over eighty families signed up to participate. I had cards printed for them to hand out that explained what the Choose Joy Project was for, directing them to my blog for more on our story.

The morning of the anniversary came quickly, and to my delight, I awoke with eagerness for what the day would bring. I wouldn't have to wait long to find out.

Early that morning I received my very first text message with a picture. A friend was at the hospital and bought someone in line breakfast then handed that person the Choose Joy card. The next message came in—someone filled up a woman's car with gas. The next message—someone gave away a free washer and dryer. Then the next—someone bought groceries for the next person in line at Walmart. On and on it went. One act after another.

I had been sifting through ideas myself and finally decided on what I would do for my Choose Joy that day. It would be threefold.

The first was simple—I bought someone's drink in the coffee line behind me. The second was simple as well—I put some cash in an envelope and put it in a lady's mailbox. She wasn't just any lady but a single mom whose yard I had helped clean up a year prior during tornado volunteer efforts. Knowing she was a single mom tugged at my heart, and I hoped she would be able to use the cash to meet her family's needs. I stuffed an envelope with cash and the card, put it in her mailbox, and made a quick getaway before she could see me. I only wish I would've gotten to see the look on her face when she went to retrieve her mail that day.

For the third act I would not go alone. I went home and picked up Milo to come along. I knew he was only two years old, but I wanted him to be a part of this day and see his daddy's life making a positive impact in the lives of others.

I buckled Milo in his car seat, and off we went to the neighborhood gas station. I let my son out and went inside to buy a gift card. We made our way back to the car and waited. I had initially hoped to see a mother with children pull up so I could make my way over to give her the card. As time wore on, I finally realized my desired demographic was nowhere to be seen. The game plan changed, and I looked for another person who needed it instead. My eyes landed on an older gentleman who I knew would be perfect.

Hopping out of the car, I took Milo and my huge pregnant belly, and we made our way toward the man. As we approached him, he looked over, quickly looking down to avoid my gaze. I am not the best at talking to complete strangers, but this mission in particular had given me all the boldness I needed.

"Hi." I walked up cheerfully.

"Um, hi," he responded, looking confused.

I shifted Milo to my other hip so I could get the card ready.

"I am out today doing random acts of kindness to honor my husband for the Choose Joy Project. I wanted to give you this," I said, handing him the Choose Joy card along with the gift card.

"This is for me?" he said, again perplexed.

"Yes, it's for you. I just wanted to bless you today," I replied.

"Are you sure?" he asked again in disbelief.

"Of course I am," I said with a laugh. "Again, I just wanted to bless you. Hope you have a great day."

I walked away quickly, leaving him there perplexed and delighted. Once we got in the car, I explained to my son what he had just witnessed.

"Milo, do you know what we just did?"

"No, Mommy," he answered honestly.

"Well, today is the anniversary of your daddy going to heaven. There was no one more amazing than your daddy. So we are doing nice things for people to honor him," I explained in a way that a two-year-old could comprehend.

"Nice things for Daddy?" he repeated.

"Yes, buddy. We were doing nice things for Daddy," I reiterated.

He said nothing more, but nothing more needed to be said. A large grin spread across his face as he leaned his head against his car seat, shut his eyes, and drifted off to sleep.

The day was a magical one. When despair could've drowned me, joy enveloped me. Hour after hour I heard unending stories of the way this project was not only changing the receivers' lives but the givers' lives as well. There is something about giving, selflessly, without expectation. That is who my husband was and what he exemplified every day. I missed him now more than ever. On that day, and every day, I had never been more proud to be his wife.

CHAPTER 8
The Arrival

The rain was coming down in buckets that morning as I awoke and looked outside. A feeling of heaviness enveloped me. Instead of eagerness, I felt dread. Grief is a difficult road to walk. You never know when a day of sorrow will hit. This day of sorrow just so happened to land on the day of my baby shower. The excitement had been building for weeks as I was preparing for this day. What I hadn't prepared for was the difficulty such an event would bring. As happy as I was to celebrate my pregnancy with my nearest and dearest, all I could think about was my last shower for Milo. Joel drove me to the event, stayed for sweet pictures with me, and then returned to gather our presents and usher me home. Once there, I showed him each adorable outfit even though he was more concerned with the practical gifts we wouldn't have to purchase ourselves. That was how it was supposed to be—him and me celebrating our baby together, not me celebrating alone.

I went to my closet and put on the lovely dress I had purchased for the occasion. I slowly curled my hair into soft waves and attempted to put on my makeup without crying. It wasn't working. I once again said a silent thank-you for waterproof mascara.

My mom and I made our way to the event despite rain flooding the streets, making the journey a bit treacherous. We arrived fifteen minutes late, adding to my already frazzled state.

The house was beautifully decorated in peach and mint. They honored my request of no pink, not a touch. I have never really been a fan of pink, and though I know it's traditional, up to that point nothing had been very traditional about my pregnancy and forthcoming baby girl. Gorgeous flower arrangements were scattered about. The food table held a massive spread of brunch food, a nod to the same menu that was served at Joel's and my wedding.

My friend and photographer greeted me at the door to take my picture. I did my best to put on the most genuine of smiles. One by one my girlfriends came over to greet me, wrapping their arms around my neck in huge hugs. They were proud of all the planning and how it had come together. I, too, was proud. Everything was lovely, well thought out, and meticulously put together. The only problem was, well, me.

Despite my best attempts, it didn't take long for them to sense I was a little off. As we gathered in the kitchen, they started to question me.

"Sarah, is everything okay?" my friend asked.

"It's not," I said, "and I don't know why. I just feel so heavy today. Not full of joy, but sadness that he's not here."

As I spoke, I started to tear up. I blinked furiously to not let the tears escape.

"I don't blame you at all," she said. "I would be sad if my husband weren't here, too."

The relief at her validation was instant. As much as they wanted me to enjoy the day, they got it. They understood this pregnancy wasn't a "normal" one. I was walking through grief and joy at the same time. With those competing emotions, joy isn't always the clear winner.

She slung her arm around me and told me the words that always cut me to the core when someone spoke them.

"Joel's proud of you, Sarah. He is. So, so proud."

I knew she was right. I knew he was proud. If we could sit down and have a conversation, he would tell me as much. Somehow, her reminder was enough to pull me out of the funk and continue on in the day. I knew her words wouldn't serve to fully pull me out of the depths I felt that day, but I hoped they would help me rise above it.

Before the close of the day, everyone gathered round to watch me open gifts. I was overwhelmed at their kindness. As I opened each gift, we all *oooohed* and *aaaaahed*. I made Joel a part of the day by telling the group which gifts he would love as well as funny stories of when we brought Milo home.

"Milo had a little bit of a reflux problem," I began. "Sure enough, every evening bottle Milo would throw up on him." They all laughed. "I would be in the other room putting on pajamas and suddenly hear a yell. '*Sarah!*' I would run in the room to find them both covered in regurgitated milk, Milo with a huge smile on his face," I remembered fondly.

I continued on opening gifts and weaving in stories. As I opened the diapers, I told them this was a Joel-approved gift. Sensible, practical. Just like he was. The thought brought a smile to my face.

It was a good day. A hard day, but a good day. The shower served as a reminder of just how much my husband was missed and still how far I had to go in not letting grief overtake me. The pull of the bitter and the sweet remained a constant. It seemed as if it would always be so.

I left the house that day with my mom and a car full of gifts. I came home to a surprise, the crib set up in the baby's room and ready to go. As I sat on the floor beside the crib, folding her little dresses, and putting her new head bows in her drawer, I was overwhelmed. It was getting real—my new best friend would be here soon.

The summer months are brutal for a pregnant woman. By the end of the day, my poor ankles looked like something out of a movie. The only things that fit were huge dresses worn with cheap flip-flops. Not exactly the epitome of put-togetherness, but I hardly cared. I was reaching the uncomfortable point where a woman's complaints increase exponentially. Thankfully my pregnancy was flying by at lightning speed. Summer was fading into fall, and I was a mere six weeks away from my daughter's arrival. I couldn't believe we were about to meet the newest member of our family in a matter of weeks. November couldn't arrive soon enough.

I had intentionally planned things out a little differently with this pregnancy. My job remained the same, working as an analyst for an oil and gas company. My position wasn't physically demanding but was mentally draining. With Milo, I had worked up to the very day I had him. I actually went to work that morning, while in labor. Life had changed this time around. I had the demands of taking care of a toddler as a single mom, while also taking care of our household and running all the necessary errands on my own. All of these factors made for an exhausting nine months.

This time I had scheduled my vacation accordingly in order to have the two weeks leading into my due date off. The forty-minute commute, each way, was getting more and more difficult to do on my own. This would allow me some downtime and much-needed rest before

I had a newborn to care for. My plan was to spend time with my son, take lots of naps, and watch lots of movies. Oh, and also to finish the nursery I had been slacking on completing.

Before I knew it, October came as did my last day of work. My coworkers came to my office to take notes of what they would cover in my absence as well as to say their good-byes. I had finished all the odds and ends; now my only duty was to wait.

Wait I did. And wait. And wait. It wasn't as if nothing was happening in the meantime. Quite the opposite. I was having contractions—and lots of them. Painful ones, too. They would come on hard and fast, going from ten minutes apart, down to nine, then eight, then seven, then six, then stop completely right before I hit the golden five-minute mark. This had gone on for weeks but started to intensify once I was home. Nearly every day I felt like it was the day I would go into full-blown labor, but my contractions continued to tease and fade away.

Soon I had my weekly check-in with my doctor. I was hoping for some major progression and the news I would soon be ready to have her.

The doctor checked me.

"Looks like you're at a one," he said firmly, in reference to my dilation.

"A one? I'm only at a measly one!" I complained. It was

really far from the necessary ten I had to reach in order to have the baby.

"Well, on the bright side, it's better than a zero," he responded.

That was no consolation. Truth was, I was anxious about labor. I was nervous it would start when no one would be nearby to take me to the hospital. Visions of driving myself to the hospital, only to stop on the side of the road and deliver my own baby, filled my head. Maybe that was a bit on the dramatic side, but the concern for the event was real.

I decided I was going to move things along as much as I could. I took the primrose pills that are supposed to start labor. I used other oils that were supposed to lend themselves to labor as well. I drank tea, ate spicy food, and walked endlessly. All those things definitely helped increase labor, no doubt. The only problem was, the labor it did start was painful and inconsistent. I was starting to have a very real understanding that this baby had a mind of her own.

I awoke on November 1 feeling as if something was different. I had been in pain all night with contractions, which was nothing new. But by the time morning approached they were holding steady. My biggest fear was going to the hospital only to be sent home, especially given that the hospital was nearly forty-five minutes away.

I was determined to wait it out as long as I could before making the trip.

The hours ticked by as I sat on the edge of my bed breathing in and then out. The contractions were as intense as they had ever been. I was ready to go to the hospital, but they still weren't close enough to do so. I remembered a nurse telling me the first time to take a bath, and that would either stop them or intensify them. I followed her advice, drawing a warm bath and staying inside until my hands were pruney. The contractions did not stop; they sped up. I wondered if this could really be the moment.

I picked up the phone and called my mom to the house, telling her I thought it might be go time. My dad came over to stay with Milo. We sat on my bed for another two hours with me in too much pain to even speak. The contractions were holding steady at five minutes apart. Finally, I'd had enough. It was time. I looked up and said the first words I had spoken to my mom in an hour.

"Mom, let's load up the car. I think it's time to have a baby."

She jumped up from my bed, running around my room frantically getting things ready to go. I worked through the pain long enough to walk out to the car, huffing and puffing through contractions as I buckled my seat belt. The pain was not letting up one bit. That is, until about fifteen minutes into the car ride.

"Oh no," I said suddenly.

"What?" my mom exclaimed, momentarily taking her eyes off the road.

"Mom, don't get us into a wreck!" I said. "It's just my contractions—it feels like they're slowing down."

"Slowing down?" she asked.

"Yes, slowing down. Should we just turn around and go home? You know I'm worried about getting all the way there only to have to come right back. . . ." My voice trailed off.

"I think we need to just keep going. Maybe you are just nervous. This has to be the real deal. I'm sure of it!" she said.

In the end we decided to keep going. A half hour later we reached the hospital. Slowly and painfully I walked the steps to the elevator. We reached the labor and delivery floor, which was quiet and calm. It seemed tonight would be the perfect night to have a baby.

I had preregistered so the intake process was swift. Before I knew it, I was in a back room waiting for a nurse to come in and check me. My labor was still dallying at that point.

Please, please, let me be in labor. Please don't let me get sent home, I thought.

The nurse entered the room and asked me numerous

questions about my contractions. Then it was time to be checked.

"It looks like you are at a. . ." She scrunched up her face. "A two."

A two. All that work and I was simply at a two. I wanted to pull out my hair in sheer frustration.

"We will keep you hooked up to the monitors for an hour. But unless there's a drastic change, I am afraid we will need to send you home," she said.

She left the room, and my face fell. My mom tried to console me that maybe the contractions would speed up again. In my heart I knew this baby girl wasn't coming tonight. My suspicions were confirmed when an hour later the nurse came in to remove the monitors and regretfully send us home.

I left the hospital one tired and frustrated mama. Thankfully I had an appointment with my doctor already scheduled for the next day.

He walked in the room, and I'm sure it was obvious that I had reached my breaking point.

"What happened?" he asked.

"I didn't get a lot of sleep last night. I was at the hospital until late, and they turned me away," I said.

"That's never fun," he responded. "Did they tell you what station you were?"

"Just a stupid two," I said with exasperation.

"Let's go ahead and check you." He did. Still a two.

The frustration bubbled to the surface, and the word *induction* was finally uttered. In talking it over with my doctor, and given the concerns about my progression, we agreed this would be the best route to take. He put me on the books for four days later. The date was set, November 6. Soon, the pain and frustration would all be over and we would have our baby girl.

The days passed quickly as I was wrapping up last-minute preparations to welcome the newest member of our family. The evening before the induction finally had come. It still felt surreal that I was about to have our daughter. Milo and I began our bedtime ritual as normal—the routine always ending with a book. As usual I let him make the book selection. He climbed up in my lap as we dived right in, slowly rocking back and forth. Milo didn't know it, but he'd picked the most poignant book we possessed to read on this most poignant night. The book spoke about new life coming into the world, how special it is, how everything changes in the most profound ways. It reinforced that each life is special, filled with purpose, and with each addition of a new little one, the world—*our* world—would never quite be the same.

Suddenly my mind was racing back to the very night Milo was born. The look of love in his father's eyes as he held his son for the very first time. The feeling of joy as

I laid eyes on my boy. The moment they placed him in my arms. The laughter and happy tears. The moment Joel kissed my head and told me how proud of me he was. That day was perfection.

My mind also went to other memories, of the last year, without Joel. We had gone from a family of three to a family of two. Milo had been my constant—my source of strength and inspiration. He gave me kisses during moments I needed them the most. The "I wuv you Mommys" were unending. He would hand me blankets when he thought I was cold and would run to protect me if he sensed I was hurt. We had made quite the little team, he and I. A lot of life had been lived in that year. Like many moms, I felt a tinge of guilt that someone else would be intruding on our sacred space. Would there be enough of me to go around? Would he resent me for bringing another person into our home? Would I be able to love as deeply as I loved this boy? I was told this was normal—to expect it. Still, the emotions of the moment were very real and very perplexing.

I returned to the task at hand, trying to get through the book without having a full-fledged Mommy breakdown moment.

Somehow I made it to the end and softly nuzzled my face to his cheek, still feeling the weight of the words I'd read.

"All done, sweet boy. Time to go to bed," I told him.

He took the book from my hands and put it away. I began to rock him to sleep. The room was dark, so he couldn't see the tears dripping down my face as I held his chubby hand and kissed his head. I closed my eyes and breathed in deeply, taking in his smell. I tried to commit every part of this moment to memory. The last moment it would ever be this way again. Milo and Mommy, quite the team we made.

༄

It's a strange feeling to wake up and know your life is going to change drastically by the day's end. That's exactly what happened as I awoke, before the sunrise, to gather my things and head to the hospital. I took one last shower so I would feel my best and grabbed my overnight bag.

On the way out I tiptoed to Milo's room, where he was still sleeping. I looked in on my baby boy, for the last time seeing him as my only child. He was snuggled in his bed under a pile of blankets, but also with his stuffed shark, giraffe, monkey, and bear. He might have been a big boy, but I would always remember him as my little baby. I took one last glance and smiled once again at the thought of how proud of him I was. I could've stayed there forever, but it was time to leave. I turned and swallowed my emotions as I closed his door and walked away. Our babysitter arrived to spend the day caring for

Milo, making me promise to call as soon as the baby had safely made her entrance into the world.

It was early, so the highways were clear as Mom and I made our way back to the hospital for the second time in six days. Luckily, this time it was for good. I walked back up to labor and delivery, where they took me to my room and instructed me to change into a hospital gown. An hour later I was hooked up to the meds and ready to get the show on the road.

The nurse started to ask me questions about my pain level, in typical hospital jargon. She kept looking around the room, and I could tell she was wondering if a father was going to be involved. As uncomfortable as it was to tell my life story to complete strangers, I knew in this instance she needed to know.

"Do you know what you're having?" she asked.

"I do, a girl," I replied.

She smiled. "Girls are wonderful."

"I'm excited for a girl. I only have experience with my little boy," I said.

She nodded her head in understanding, and I knew I had my in.

"There's a very incredible story about how she came to be. Would you like to hear it?" I asked her.

"Of course," she quickly said.

"Well, my husband and I had trouble conceiving, so we

used IVF to get pregnant with my son. After he was born, my husband's cancer returned, and he passed away last summer. The amazing thing is we still had these embryos left. I went ahead and decided to put them in and leave it up to the Lord. I ended up getting pregnant, with this very baby girl," I said in a nutshell. The words sounded so simple as they left my mouth, though the reality had been anything but.

It was a huge bomb to drop on anyone, much less a nurse in these circumstances. Her jaw was nearly on the floor.

"That's the most incredible thing I've ever heard," she said, looking shocked.

"Her daddy won't be here, but a piece of him is coming into the world today, and I'm so blessed I get to meet her," I said emotionally.

She took my hand, and like many others, she told me she thought I was brave. Again, I thought not so, just blessed.

⁓

The medicine worked quickly. Within the first hour my contractions were already at two to three minutes apart. I asked for the epidural, only to be told the anesthesiologist was in another delivery and I would have to wait. By the time he arrived, two hours later, I was ready to rip someone's head off. The contractions were so painful I could hardly sit still for him to do his job. Thankfully he worked fairly quickly. Around thirty minutes later, the drugs took effect and I started to relax.

The day wore on, as hour after hour they would come to check me. Each time I was progressing another centimeter, then another, then another. It was moving at a snail's pace, but it was moving. By three o'clock that afternoon, it was time for another check. My doctor entered the room.

"Let's see where things stand," he said.

He started to check me and then got a serious look on his face.

"The good news is you're at a ten. The bad news is the baby's head is turned in the wrong position. We are going to have to wait to see if the baby's head will turn so you can deliver."

I was frustrated beyond belief. I was right where I needed to be, and feeling the urge to push, but I was told to wait. This felt like it would never end. To make matters worse, my doctor had a prior commitment that evening and would not be able to stay late to deliver my daughter. The on-call doctor, a man I had never met, would take over his duties. This baby was going to come on her own time, and apparently no one was going to rush her.

The nurse put me in different positions, moving me around to try to get the baby in the proper place. They kept checking me and telling me over and over I wasn't ready to push. Two hours later, I knew the time had come. Whether they wanted me to or not, there was no holding back.

I hit the button for the nurse, and she came rushing in.

"I need you to check me again. I think I'm ready," I said in sheer exhaustion.

She obliged and checked me.

"The baby's head still isn't in the right position," she determined.

"I can't hold back any longer. I have to push. I feel so much pressure. I have to," I said desperately.

"Okay," she said. "When the next contraction comes, I will tell you and we can do a few practice pushes."

I nodded my head vigorously and closed my eyes, waiting for her instructions.

"All right, now push. One, two, three, four, five, six, seven, eight, nine, ten. One more time! One, two, three, four, five, six, seven, eight, nine, ten!"

I paused to take a breath and get ready to go again.

"Wait!" she exclaimed. "Stop!"

I looked down at her to see what was going on.

"The baby's head is almost out! I have to go get the doctor. Whatever you do, don't push!" she cried.

She ran out the door to get the doctor. Within minutes the entire room was filled with medical personnel getting the room ready for delivery. The doctor appeared and told me to push. Everything was moving quickly. A mere two pushes in, the doctor was encouraging me: "One more push and you are going to be a mommy," he said.

I stopped and took every bit of that moment in. I was about to meet her. My miracle baby. In my mind I whispered my thanks to the Lord. There was one more person I had words for as well.

JoJo, I love you. I love you, I thought.

"Okay, it's time. Push!" the doctor yelled.

I took a deep breath in and did just that. Silence. Then wails. A cry. Her cry. A piece of our love had entered the world. Joel's and my little girl.

"We will have a girl," Joel had told me. *"You know what to name her."*

I did. Ellis Claire Rodriguez. Her name means "a bright shining light, declaring Jehovah is God."

"She's here! You have a little baby girl!" the doctor said.

They cleaned her off and placed her on my chest, skin to skin. She was crying loudly, signaling her arrival to the world. I looked down at her mess of dark hair and big brown eyes. She was beautiful, just beautiful. She looked like her daddy. I've never seen a more adorable little lady. I was in love. Immediately my heart expanded in ways I never knew it could. Death had visited us and so cruelly ripped away a part of our family. Yet she brought life and beauty to our ashes. For our mourning, she was now our joy, a bright light to the world, showing the goodness of the Lord in the midst of despair.

I looked at her and cried as she continued to cry. I wrapped my arms around her, holding her close, pulling her in for comfort. The crying eventually stopped as she nestled in and breathed deeply. Then something incredible happened. She reached up with her tiny little hand and grabbed my favorite necklace—the one with her daddy's and brother's fingerprints. She held on to it tightly, as if she would never let go. That moment signified to me that we were a family of four. Joel, me, Milo, and Ellis. Only a few minutes old, she already seemed to grasp that fact. It was as if she was telling me she already knew and understood the significance—that she was there to add to our story, and in no way take away from my relationship with Milo. She might never meet Joel on this earth, but she knew he was a part of her, and that he loved her in every way. I reached up and held her hand, encircling mine around the necklace as well. Then I reached down and kissed the face of my gorgeous baby girl.

All who met her over the next few hours marveled at her beauty. There was no mistaking her physical beauty, yes, but even more the beauty of her story. As much as I loved showing her off, she still hadn't met the most important person on the list: Milo.

She got her chance the following day. She hadn't slept

much the night before—and neither had I. She had cried off and on the entire evening until I finally held her in my arms, where she slept through the rest of the night peacefully. She might look like her daddy, but already I could tell she was strong and determined to have her way, much like her mama.

I sat on the bed with her, waiting for my family to arrive. I was a little worried about how this moment would play out. I'd had many conversations with Milo about Ellis. I had tried to ramp up the excitement level, to no avail. Most of our conversations went like this: "Milo, you will have a baby sister soooooooon! Are you *excited*?" I would ask in a high-pitched voice.

"No," he would say. "I don't want it."

An *it*. Baby sister was an it. This wasn't going well. A few weeks later, I would try again.

"What's that?" Milo would ask, pointing to my rapidly growing belly.

"Buddy, that's your baby sister. You get to meet her soon. Isn't that fun!"

"No," he would say once again. "I just don't want it."

That was his typical refrain the entire pregnancy. I was a little worried about what this meeting would hold for us. I would soon find out.

I heard a small knock on the door.

"Come in!" I yelled.

In walked Milo, dressed in an adorable sweater and jeans. He was holding a love offering for his new sister, a precious little furry white lamb. I looked at her, then him, hardly believing he had ever been this small. Overnight he looked as if he had become a little man. My heart both ached and soared.

"Milo, this is who I've been telling you about. This is your baby sister," I said. "You are a big brother now!"

He walked over to my bed and peered down at this new little person, taking it all in. There was a moment of nervous energy as everyone in the room waited to see what he would say.

Slowly, a huge smile crept across his face.

"Can I hold her?" he asked.

"Of course you can," I responded in relief.

My mom lifted Ellis out of my arms and directed Milo to a chair. We placed a pillow under his arms for support. Then, ever so carefully, she placed Ellis in her brother's arms. He looked down at her, studying every bit of her face.

"This is my baby sister?" he asked again in disbelief.

"Yes, it is," I answered.

"Aw, she's so cute! I love my baby sister," he said enthusiastically.

Then, he reached down, and as soft as he could muster, he kissed her face. He looked up at me with a smile so big my heart could burst. Relief. He loved her. Already his heart had opened and welcomed her into his space. I looked at my children, two of them, and I couldn't believe it. All the years of pain over my inability to conceive. All the moments of fears and questions. All the wondering, would I ever be a mom? Would my dream ever come true? For so long it had mocked me, and now it embraced me. Indeed, this life was mine.

CHAPTER 9
Don't Let Her Go

I still can't believe she's here, I thought as I looked down at Ellis, all cozy and cuddled in her blanket, strapped into her car seat.

Her beauty still took my breath away—even days later. The first week home with a baby is like a fog. You are in pure survival mode. Keep the baby changed, fed, and happy. If you are lucky, you might be able to fit in a few hours of sleep for yourself. And showers? Well, those become a luxury. Everything takes a backseat to this tiny thing that just graced your world. The funny thing is you wouldn't have it any other way.

The day we brought her home was the first day I would dress in actual clothes and head out to the real world. During the first week, I had help from my mom and our sitter during the day, but evenings were all my own, and like all new moms I was exhausted from lack of sleep. We went on our first outing since leaving the hospital, a routine check-in with Ellis's pediatrician. It was a quick in and out, mostly to check her weight and make sure she wasn't losing too much, as is typical for some newborns. The pediatrician looked her over and told me she was perfect. Perfect. Those are the words every new mother wants to hear.

My dad was driving us that day since I was still on postbaby driving restriction. As we drove home, I was thinking about hospitals and doctor's appointments. I didn't like them. Not at all. And though my birthing and pediatric experience was pleasant, I still wish I never had to step foot in any medical institution ever. In Joel's battle with cancer, we had been in far too many hospitals. I felt like I had met my quota for the rest of my life. It represented some of my life's most painful moments, not just physically but emotionally as well. Even though my last hospital experience was the joyful arrival of my little girl, I still didn't feel comfortable in one.

"Dad," I started in, "I hate hospitals."

"Okay. . . ," he said, waiting for the rest of my remarks.

"It's just that Joel has been gone for a year and a half. And in that year and a half, it's been nice to not have to battle for a life, going from hospital to hospital," I said.

He nodded in understanding.

"Don't get me wrong, I would gladly sit at a hospital all day long just to have Joel back with me. I would never trade what I have for no hospitals. But I will just say, that if there's one small silver lining, it's that I haven't had to spend so much time in hospitals. I hope I never, ever have to do that again. It's horrible," I told him.

"Well, that's certainly understandable. You've had quite the journey the past few years," he agreed as a front-row witness to it all.

Merely a week later, those very words would come back to haunt me. In a big, big way.

∼

That night was like most nights with a newborn—Ellis wasn't interested in sleep. I could rock her, swing her, jostle her, nothing worked. She didn't want her bed, and she didn't want her swing. The only thing she wanted was my arms. So I held her most of the evening, trying to calm the fussiness and get her to drift off to sleep.

By 7:00 a.m. I was finally able to calm her down and get her to rest in the swing in my bedroom. By 7:30 my babysitter came in to get her and take her to the living room so I could finally get some sleep. I lay down in my bed, exhausted from the long evening, and was excited to close my eyes and drift off. It didn't last long.

Thirty minutes later my door swung open, and my babysitter flew in in a panic.

"Sarah," she said. "Wake up! There's something wrong with Ellis!"

I sat up quickly, completely disoriented as to what was happening. She had never before run into my room and woken me up like that. I had also never before seen the look that was on her face. I pride myself in being calm in emergency situations, and this was no different. I tried to quickly assess what was going on and calm my babysitter down.

"What is wrong, Kaylee?" I asked her.

"I don't know what's wrong with her. She has been wincing in pain nonstop, and she feels warm to me. Really warm," she said, her voice rising.

I reached over and took Ellis from her arms, quickly putting my hand to her forehead. She was right—she felt warm. My mind went back to the pediatrician's office the week before.

"For a baby, any temperature over 100.1 degrees is an emergency," she had told me sternly.

I looked over at my clock. It was only 8:00 a.m. The doctor's office would not open for another thirty minutes.

"Go get the thermometer," I directed her.

She raced in the room and came right back. I pushed the thermometer to Ellis's head—99 degrees. I tried it again—98.9. I tried it again—100. Her reading was dancing all over the place.

"It's okay, Kaylee," I said, trying to calm her down. "She's going to be okay. I'm going to call the pediatrician and get her in today. Don't worry."

I was trying not to worry myself.

At 8:30 a.m. on the dot I called the pediatrician and

was, of course, directed to a nurse.

"What's her temp?" she asked.

"I can't get a straight reading. It keeps changing on me," I replied.

"Have you taken her temp rectally?" she asked.

"No, I haven't," I said.

She instructed me to go find our digital thermometer and take her temperature that way as it was the most reliable.

I ran to the medicine cabinet and found the thermometer. I placed it under her armpit first and took it that way—99 degrees. Next I checked it rectally—100 degrees. I grabbed my phone and called the nurse back, telling her of the conclusion.

"It sounds like she's not quite to the danger zone. It's your call if you want to go ahead and bring her in." She put the ball in my court.

I looked down at Ellis. She was sleeping now, but off and on she would wince in pain. I couldn't quite tell, but it also looked as if she was getting a little pale. As much as I would prefer to just treat an illness at home, my gut told me this might be serious.

"I think I would like to go ahead and bring her in, just to be on the safe side," I told them.

They put me down for the first open slot—one o'clock that afternoon.

I spent the time until then holding Ellis. Her fussiness was growing by the hour. She had taken her morning bottles, but by the afternoon, she no longer seemed interested. I was glad one o'clock came quickly. Still exhausted from being up over twenty-four hours with no sleep, I'd hoped the doctor's visit would be quick—that I could get Ellis to lie down and get some sleep myself.

We arrived at the pediatrician's, and they swooped us back to a room. The nurse took her temperature via the armpit—99 degrees. I let out a sigh of relief. Hopefully I was just imagining things, and they would send us on home. My worst fear was a trip to the ER, all on my own.

The doctor came in a few moments later, took Ellis from my arms, and laid her on the examining table.

"Does she look pale to you?" she asked me immediately.

"I was kind of thinking that she did," I answered truthfully.

She took out her thermometer and placed it in Ellis's rectum. It beeped, signaling the results were in. She looked at the reading, scrunching up her face.

"One hundred point one," she said.

My face fell. I knew what that meant.

"Sarah, I'm sorry to say this, but I am going to have to send you to the ER. I am going to make a call and tell them you are on your way. Don't go home first, don't stop for anything—go straight there," she said, her voice serious. She didn't tell me what she thought was happening then, but later on I found out she had her suspicions immediately that Ellis was a very sick little girl.

"Okay," I said simply. I felt the fear rising and the tears threatening to come along with it.

This was every mother's fear, taking a two-week-old baby to the hospital because something was wrong. It was especially difficult in my circumstance—without my Joel. I was terrified.

The doctor had me quickly pack Ellis up in her car seat and head over to the local hospital. On my way there, I desperately tried to calm my nerves. I told myself over and over again it was going to be okay. *Things like this happen—it's not going to be a big deal.* As much as I tried to convince myself that was the case, I couldn't help but feel it was far more serious. Things were happening at such a rapid pace; I knew it could be something really bad. My intuition rarely failed me. Deep inside I had that same foreboding feeling that life was taking another devastating turn.

The ride to the hospital was over before I knew it. I pulled into the entrance labeled ER in bright red letters. Thankfully the lobby was empty and the intake was swift. They took Ellis, put her on the table, and started to put in an IV so they could take her labs. As they worked, I frantically texted my family and friends to tell them what was happening, asking them to pray. Not long after, my mom was able to leave work and join us. I was so thankful to no longer be alone. The relief was short lived when I saw the concern on my mom's face as she looked Ellis over.

It took over an hour for them to get an IV in her tiny little veins. Baby veins weren't made for IVs—they also weren't made for hospitals.

An emergency room pediatrician came in the room and told us all the tests they were going to run on her. When they got to a spinal tap, my stomach turned.

"Whoa, whoa, whoa, a spinal tap? On a brand-new baby?" I said in shock.

"Yes," she answered. "We always like to rule out meningitis. I know it sounds scary, but it's necessary. Don't worry, Mom, most likely it's RSV, and you all will be out of here within forty-eight hours or so."

I felt like all the air was gone from the room. I was terrified for my daughter, who by that point seemed to be getting more and more pale. She also seemed to be more lethargic, not even crying in pain as they continuously poked her small frame with needles.

Another doctor came in the room and told me he was going to start the spinal tap procedure. He listed out all the bad things that could happen but told me the test was still necessary. He advised me to wait in the waiting room down the hall since it might be difficult for me to watch. My mom volunteered to stay in the room with Ellis. He walked me down the hall to the room and told me he would be back in about forty-five minutes or so.

I sat in the chair and pulled out my phone, replying to incoming messages from my friends desperate to know what was happening. It was then I heard a scream from what I thought was the doctor's voice.

"Mooooooooooooooooooom!" the voice yelled.

Surely that couldn't be for me. It had to be for someone else. I sat still in my chair, hearing footsteps charging toward the room. My room. The voice calling for a mother was calling for me.

A moment later and the doctor was in the room, practically pulling me up from the chair and back to Ellis's room.

"Mom, there's an emergency. When I turned her on her side to start the test, she went blue and almost stopped breathing. We have her on oxygen now and are going to have to transfer her to Children's in Oklahoma City—just in case she needs to be on a vent," he said with urgency.

Wait? What? A vent? What was happening right now? What was going on with my daughter? I felt disoriented and confused.

"I'm going to call a transport team. We are going to take her in an ambulance with lights and sirens," he said.

I walked beside him, silently, in absolute shock. We finally reached her room and I saw my sweet girl with oxygen connected to her face. They were loading her up in her car seat and putting her on an ambulance gurney. My mom's face was white as a sheet. My heart was aching.

"I am going to follow behind the ambulance. I will call Dad, and we will meet you there," she said.

They loaded her up in the ambulance with me in the front seat. I could hear the wail of the sirens as they peeled out of the hospital, heading north up the interstate to Children's Hospital.

We have all seen ambulances pass by us before, sirens and lights blaring. It was surreal to be the one inside the ambulance as we sped up the highway, cars veering to get out of our way. As we got closer and closer, my prayers became more and more frantic.

"I don't know what's going on, Lord, but please be with my girl," I said in my feeble attempt to find words in this moment.

The terror inside my heart was rising. This was unreal. She had to be okay. She just had to be okay. I was vacillating between disbelief and shock. How could this be happening again? Another life-threatening situation in the midst of what was supposed to be a celebration of life.

We took our exit off the highway, barreling toward the hospital. The driver took the first right, and we were a block away. I looked out the window and saw a familiar building, the main hospital where my husband died. Suddenly, I was furious. I had lost him not even two years ago. Now, I had Ellis in an ambulance on oxygen because she couldn't breathe. What was happening, and why was it happening to us? Hadn't we been through enough? That same feeling of dread was rising just as it had with Joel, and I shoved it down as far as I could.

They pulled into the back entrance of Children's Hospital and rushed the gurney into the ER. I followed closely behind. My mom and dad stood by my side, seemingly appearing out of thin air. No one said a word.

We got back to a room in the ER as the transport team handed her charts over to the ER team. A male nurse took Ellis out of her car seat and placed her on a table. She was lethargic and barely moving. One look at her and he ran to the intercom.

"I need a doctor in here *now!*" he yelled.

The room instantly filled up with no fewer than ten people, all running around the table that held the small, fragile body of my baby girl. I instinctively backed out of their way while not taking my eyes off her. The commotion was frantic. I felt as if I was going to faint. Someone came over and told me she had nearly stopped breathing again, and she needed to be placed on a ventilator if she was going to live.

Not a vent. Anything but a vent, I thought.

Memories were swirling, racing through my head of her daddy on a vent. Begging for a miracle. Removing her daddy from a vent. Saying good-bye. No, no, no, this could not be. She was our miracle baby, and it seemed cruel that this part of Joel might now be taken from me, too. It was more than I could bear. Her struggling to breathe? I thought of her dad struggling to breathe on a vent. He was an adult who had lived a full life; she was a helpless baby at the very beginning of hers. She never even had a chance.

There was no other choice but to sign my name to the sheet of paper being forced under my nose. The tears blinded my eyes as I, once again, made a horrific but necessary decision to save the life of my loved one.

Within minutes, the room was filled with even more people as the tube was inserted down her throat and the vent turned on. I looked at the clock. It was 7:00 p.m. It had been a mere eleven hours since my babysitter had stormed into my room saying something was wrong. Now my precious daughter was on a ventilator, clinging to life. I still couldn't comprehend it.

The room finally emptied, and I could walk over to her bed. I looked at her all covered in wires, the beeps and chimes going off. Unfortunately I knew from prior experience what all the numbers on the machines meant. I looked up at the monitors and saw that her blood pressure was high, her heart rate even higher. I took her little hand in mine, not believing what was happening. Once again, it seemed like a bad dream. I wanted to take her and run out the door.

One of my girlfriends showed up and came in the room, putting her arm around my shoulders. She noticed my legs were weakening and gently guided me to a chair. I collapsed in sobs.

The doctors came back and told me tests had revealed my Ellis had bacterial meningitis and was in septic shock. I had no idea what any of it meant. I had heard of meningitis before and knew it was serious, but I hadn't known it regularly took the lives of babies, as my doctor explained to me. I remembered our babysitter had had meningitis before and recovered from it just fine. I figured it was something Ellis would quickly recover from and be home in no time. I had no clue there might not be any going home. I wouldn't let myself go there. I couldn't. I refused to believe there would be anything less than a full recovery. My heart could accept no other fate.

They told me they were going to transfer Ellis to the PICU, and I could follow her up. Once we got to the floor, we met the PICU doctor. She told us they were going to put a central line in Ellis that would allow them to access her vein easily for numerous medications. I should have known then this would not be a quick hospitalization.

They sent us to the waiting room for what they said would be a short procedure to put in the line. By that time a few hours had passed. I'd sent my mom home to be with Milo, to keep things normal at the house and relieve the babysitter. My dad and I, along with my girlfriend, sat and waited for the procedure to end.

"Sarah, did I tell you about the woman from downstairs?" she said.

I shook my head, confused. "No. . .what woman?"

"Well, when we were downstairs, this random woman came up to me, pointed to Ellis, and asked me if it was my baby. I told her no, it was my friend's baby. The lady looked in the room at Ellis and said, 'That baby's going to be all right. God just told me, she's going to be all right.' The funny thing is, this woman appeared from nowhere. She even had gold teeth! But she was so sure when she said it. It was like she knew something we didn't," she said.

It wasn't much, but it was something I could cling to. *That baby's going to be all right.* God had told a stranger my baby was going to be all right. She had to be.

An hour had passed, then two hours. We were still in the room, waiting for them to finish her line. I knew something was wrong. I could feel it in my gut. It shouldn't be taking this long.

Finally, a resident came out to speak with us. She asked me for a rundown of the morning and what had led us to the current events. I went over them methodically. Woke up with a slight temperature. Was cranky. Went to the doctor, who sent us to the ER. She nearly stopped breathing there, so they sent us here. That was it. No other symptoms or any warning signs that would lead us to where we were now.

"Ellis is a very sick little baby. You just need to know that. She's a very sick girl," she said to me seriously.

I was irritated as she stated the obvious. Granted, most normal families would need to be talked to in simple terms. This, however, was no normal family. We had been through a three-year journey, ending with a six-week nightmare with Joel. I knew what a vent was and what it meant. And I knew it was bad if she was sick enough to be placed on one.

They led us back to Ellis's room, where she was hooked up to even more wires and already on several medications to help steady her vitals. I looked at the top of her head and could see a bump where it was starting to swell. The doctor saw me staring and led me to a chair at the back of her room. She knelt beside me.

"Ellis is very sick. Do you see that bump on her head?"

I nodded silently.

"That is her brain swelling. The meningitis is attacking

her brain," she said matter-of-factly.

I wanted to curl up in a ball and weep.

"I need to know what the extent of the damage is. We need to take her down for a CT scan," she said.

It was then I started sobbing uncontrollably. Not a CT scan. No! Her daddy had CT scans. Hundreds of them. It was always bad news. Devastating news. I couldn't even think about my little baby going in to have a CT scan. It was beyond understanding.

I was shaking and sobbing hard as my dad explained to the doctor about my reaction, telling her about Joel, telling her our story. The doctor shook her head in disbelief.

"This is just like what happened with Joel," I said, nearly screaming. "It's just like it!"

Everyone in the room was silent. I was wrapped in a hospital blanket yet still trembling in shock. The doctor looked at the ground, trying in vain to formulate her next answer. Words seemed to be failing her; then again, they seemed to be failing us all.

"I'm so sorry. I'm just so sorry. I wish there was another way, but I have to find out what's going on with her. I promise you that she needs it. I wouldn't have her get a scan if I didn't think it was necessary. She needs it. Do I have your permission?" she asked.

Again, I felt as if I was betraying my family member by consenting, yet there was no other choice. I was shaking and weeping, on the verge of hysterics with worry. Ellis was our joy for mourning, our beauty from ashes, and now she was in the PICU on death's door. Life seemed unfathomably cruel.

They came to load up all the equipment to take her away for her scan. I stood beside her bed, holding her hand, telling her I loved her and it was going to be okay. Flashbacks filled my mind of this same thing happening with Joel. Could this really be happening with our daughter, too? I gently stroked her face and kissed her little fingers. I didn't know how I would ever be able to let her go. Before I knew it the time had arrived, and they were prepared to leave.

God, please, don't let her go. Please don't let my baby girl go. Please, I said in silent prayer as they slowly wheeled her away.

Top: The very first picture Joel and I took together. We were lovebirds already by that point. *(Photo: Sarah Rodriguez)* **Left:** Our first dance together as husband and wife. One of the greatest days of my life. *(Photo: Sarah Rodriguez)* **Right:** The mountains were one of our favorite places to be. Here we are a few years into our marriage, in the thick of our battle with infertility. *(Photo: Sarah Rodriguez)*

RIGHT: After completing our first half-marathon, a bucket list goal for each of us. Joel was diagnosed with cancer a few weeks later. *(Photo: Sarah Rodriguez)*

BELOW: Joel about to have surgery to remove his kidney and the cancer that had engulfed it. Still smiling, ever the brave one. *(Photo: Sarah Rodriguez)*

BOTTOM RIGHT: Deep into chemo treatments, bald head and all. We were in a battle for his life and holding tight to each other like never before. *(Photo: So Darn Happy Photography)*

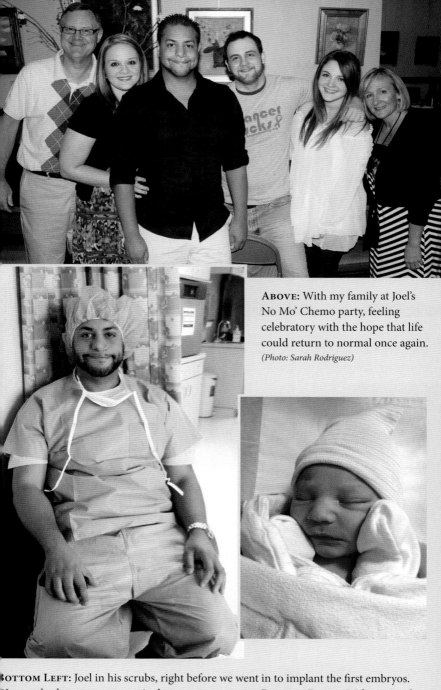

ABOVE: With my family at Joel's No Mo' Chemo party, feeling celebratory with the hope that life could return to normal once again. *(Photo: Sarah Rodriguez)*

BOTTOM LEFT: Joel in his scrubs, right before we went in to implant the first embryos. We were both nervous, yet excited. *(Photo: Sarah Rodriguez)* **BOTTOM RIGHT:** Welcome to the world, Milo Andrew Rodriguez. Our dream come true. *(Photo: Sarah Rodriguez)*

ABOVE: The photo I snapped the morning of Joel's surgery, the last time my boys would ever be together as they were. I wish I could've frozen this moment. *(Photo: Sarah Rodriguez)*

LEFT: At Milo's baby dedication, a few weeks before Joel's second surgery to remove the spreading cancer from his lung. *(Photo: Sarah Rodriguez)* **BELOW:** Yet another new normal, wheeling Joel down the rehab halls. *(Photo: Deisy Photography)*

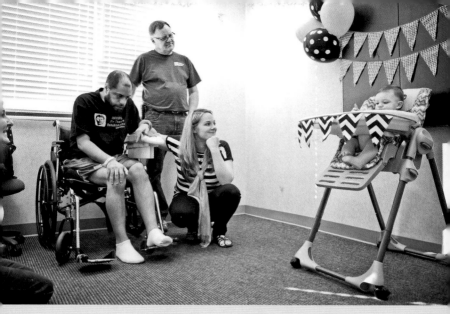

ABOVE: Celebrating Milo's first birthday at the rehab center. This was the last time we were ever together as a family. The day was extremely bittersweet. *(Photo: Deisy Photography)*
BELOW: The morning of Joel's funeral with his best friends from left to right—Simon, Pierre, Me, Milo, Jorge, and Russ. Smiling on the outside because they are there, wrecked on the inside because Joel is not. *(Photo: Sarah Rodriguez)*

LEFT: After Joel's funeral was over, releasing balloons into the sky in honor of his 36th birthday that was only 3 weeks away. Forever 35. *(Photo: Mary Morrow)*

FAR RIGHT: With my mom moments before I went in to have the last remaining embryos implanted. *(Photo: Sarah Rodriguez)* **RIGHT:** Welcome to the world, Ellis Claire Rodriguez. A miracle from the start. *(Photo: Sarah Rodriguez)*

BELOW: For our mourning He gave us joy. *(Photo: Magnolia Adams Photography)*

LEFT: Our first night in the PICU. This was before the horrific swelling in her brain began to manifest. So many cords and tubes on such a tiny little baby. *(Photo: Sarah Rodriguez)*

FAR LEFT: The first moments after Ellis was removed from the vent and placed on my chest. Weeping as I held her in my arms and choked out my goodbyes. *(Photo: Sarah Rodriguez)*

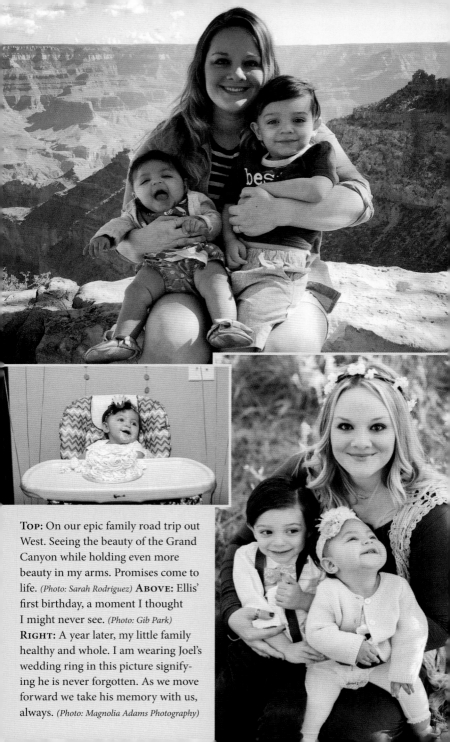

Top: On our epic family road trip out West. Seeing the beauty of the Grand Canyon while holding even more beauty in my arms. Promises come to life. *(Photo: Sarah Rodriguez)* **Above:** Ellis' first birthday, a moment I thought I might never see. *(Photo: Gib Park)* **Right:** A year later, my little family healthy and whole. I am wearing Joel's wedding ring in this picture signifying he is never forgotten. As we move forward we take his memory with us, always. *(Photo: Magnolia Adams Photography)*

CHAPTER 10
My Sunshine

"Ms. Rodriguez," I thought I heard a loud voice say to my left. I awoke momentarily. The voice seemed to go away, so I started to drift off again.

"Ms. Rodriguez!" said the voice more firmly this time.

A hand was now tapping my hip. I awoke and turned to my left side, totally exhausted and completely disoriented. I blinked hard, trying to wake up my body and get my bearings. Now it was sinking in. I was in the PICU with Ellis. This was a doctor trying furiously to awaken me. Unfortunately, it hadn't all been a bad dream.

I sat up in my bed to face her.

"Ellis's platelets are extremely low. We need you to sign off on a form for us to give her more," she was saying.

I wiped the sleep from my eyes as I heard her rattling off all the risks and benefits. Then she shoved a pen and paper in my hand to sign. I glanced up at the clock. It was 4:00 a.m. After almost two days without sleep, I had drifted off, only getting in a measly hour before I was awakened.

A few hours prior they had taken Ellis back for a CT

scan that showed the swelling had started in her brain. Her vitals were going crazy, up and down like a roller coaster. She was on four different medications just to keep them stable. All evening long the monitors would go off and nurses would rush in the room to attend to her.

They had her in a medically induced coma to allow her body to rest. Because of that, I couldn't see the seizures that had begun wracking her body due to the instability in her brain. They eventually hooked her up to an EEG machine, which would monitor them. She now had little prongs fastened to every inch of her skull. Every other part of her body was covered in cords and lines. The only part of her I could kiss that wasn't covered in medical equipment was one of her little legs. I could also put my finger in her tiny hand.

The medical staff recommended the parent not leave the child, which is good because I had no plans to do so. At the far corner of the room was a futon with a plastic padding. I covered it in hospital sheets and made it my bed. It was terribly uncomfortable but pretty much what you would expect from a hospital. I had our sitter and my family staying with Milo, trying to keep things as normal as possible for him. Only a day in, and I missed him terribly.

The following morning was one of the moments I looked forward to the least—doctors' rounds. On one hand you want to know more information about your loved one, but on the other hand, all the details they give you tend to lean toward the negative. When you are clinging to hope, you want someone to give you something, anything, to keep you going. I learned early on I wasn't going to be getting it from a doctor. Our particular hospital was a teaching hospital, which means it was not only the doctor who came in the room but typically an entourage of four to six others. It can be quite the intimidating scene.

"Hello," the doctor said as he strolled in the room.

"Hi," I answered softly.

"I'll start with the facts. She is still very sick and in critical condition. As you can tell, and the scans showed, she has pretty severe brain swelling. Because of that she's having seizures. Her vitals aren't very stable, so we have her on several meds to help with that. We haven't really been able to stabilize her much, though, despite all these meds, and things are still up and down. We won't even be able to think of feeding her for quite a while because her body can't handle it."

I nodded. All this I knew.

"Overall prognosis: not good. Meningitis hits small babies like this pretty hard. Most of the time many won't survive. If they do, they typically aren't able to walk, talk, see, or hear," he said bluntly.

The doctor had just given me the worst news you

would want to hear about your child. I now had no fewer than six pairs of eyes staring at me, awaiting my response.

"Well, Doctor, I appreciate your medical analysis. But I am a person of faith, and I believe in miracles. Say what you want, but I believe God is going to heal my baby girl," I said resolutely.

The doctor seemed slightly taken aback at my response. In the far corner a nurse caught my eye, and ever so slightly she smiled and nodded her head in encouragement.

"There are always miracles that can happen, I suppose," he said, shrugging. "Do you have any other questions?" he asked.

I could tell he was ready to leave, which was good because I was ready for him to leave.

"No, thank you," I replied.

The staff shuffled out the door, and I was left alone with my girl. I walked over to her little bed.

"Ellis, you don't pay any mind to what they say about you. You are a fighter, and you are going to beat this. God is going to heal you. You just rest, baby girl," I told her. I kissed her leg and walked back to my bed.

The tears started to fall. I was trying to stay strong—strong in front of them and strong for her. Yet, deep down I was afraid. I didn't know if God would heal her. My mind was still reeling from the events only sixteen months prior: Joel on a vent after numerous strokes. I believed then with my whole heart and nothing less that God would heal him. No one could convince me otherwise. I shouted it from the rooftops and fiercely held on to my belief until his death. I didn't know where that left my belief in miracles. Do they ever really happen? Why did God not heal my husband? I had no answers. Yet, I remembered in the Bible a verse about having faith the size of a mustard seed and that you could move mountains with that kind of faith.

Wait! A thought occurred to me. I remembered Ellis's nursery at our house. I had spent months decorating it. I am not girly, or frilly, so it took a while to decide on the decor. In the end I chose beige, ivories, chocolate browns, and gold. Her room was lovely, feminine, but not over the top. I knew I had wanted a sign for her wall that was a declaration for her life. I scoured the Internet for different themes and ideas. One finally jumped out at me, and I knew it was for Ellis. I commissioned a friend to create a sign for me with the quote and hung it over her bed. The quote stated, WHEN SHE WAKES, SHE WILL MOVE MOUNTAINS.

My mustard seed of faith was all I had, but it was going to have to move the mountains until my girl woke up from her coma and started to move them herself. It was another small thing to hold on to, but with my faith running low, I would take every small thing I could.

We were almost to the one-week mark, and Ellis was mostly the same. The meningitis was still attacking her body unmercifully. By this time she was up to seven different medications, four to keep her vitals steady and three to help with seizures alone. Even with all the different meds, the EEG was showing she was having seizures every few minutes. Everything was so unstable, and day after day I was told the same news: things are looking bleak, but we will just have to watch and see.

I hadn't left the hospital once. I was missing my favorite boy deeply, and after a week apart, I knew I had to see him. It was also the day before my favorite holiday, Thanksgiving. My heart was aching over the fact we wouldn't be together as a family to celebrate it. My spirits were at an all-time low when my mom decided to bring Milo to the hospital to see me. I didn't want him to see his sister in her current condition, so Mom offered to sit with her while I took Milo to the park on the sixth floor of the hospital. I was so excited all morning to finally get to see my son yet anxious about being away from Ellis, even though it was only two floors away.

My phone rang, and it was my mom telling me they were outside the PICU. I kissed Ellis, telling her I would be back soon. I slowly walked out of her room, momentarily overwhelmed by the sunshine shining brightly in the halls. I saw my family from the back, about twenty feet away. I could recognize those dark curls anywhere.

"Milo!" I yelled.

He turned around and saw me. A huge smile crept across his face.

"Mooooooommmmmmmy!" he yelled, turning to run to me.

I stepped forward and caught him in my arms. His hug was fierce as he was giving me kisses all over my face. There had never been a more beautiful reunion. I had missed him so deeply.

"Mommy, I love you," he said sweetly. This boy had every bit of me wrapped around his tiny little fingers.

"I love you, too, bubs. I'm so, so happy you came to see me. Are you ready to go to the playground?" I asked.

He nodded his head enthusiastically.

"Okay, let's go," I said.

I hugged my Mom good-bye as she hit the buzzer to be let back to the PICU with Ellis. She handed over a picnic lunch for us to share. I grabbed Milo's hand, and we walked to the elevators that would take us to the playground.

We made our way outside to a thankfully mild November day. It was my first time in over a week not to breathe hospital air. I set up shop for us off to the side of the playground, spreading out our blanket and unloading the food. Milo is always happiest when food is involved, so he dived right in.

"Mommy, I miss you," he said.

"I miss you, too, buddy. I do," I said, my heart breaking.

"You are staying at the hospital with baby sister?" he asked.

"Yes. I have been here with her this whole time," I answered.

"Mommy, are you and my baby sister going to come home soon?" he responded.

"I hope so, buddy. I really, really hope so," I said.

At that moment I wished there were two of me—one to stay at the hospital fighting for my daughter and the other to go home and love on my son. I was trying so hard to be both things for both children, and in the end, I still felt like it wasn't enough.

"I'm praying for baby sister, that God would make her much better," he said.

Trying not to cry, I reached over and pushed a little strand of his hair out of his eyes. I leaned in and gave him a huge hug. I tried desperately not to allow the anger of what we were enduring to overshadow our moments together, but it was incredibly hard. In only two years of life, this little boy had already been through so much. I'd thought about it before, but I thought it again: life can certainly be unfair.

My thoughts were interrupted by a loud squeal and

Milo grabbing my hand.

"Mommy, let's go play!" he yelled.

The deep thoughts, worries, and fears would have to wait. For now, it was time to simply play with my most favorite little boy.

❧

We were now almost to the two-week mark of being in the hospital. Friends and family had kept a constant vigil by my side, and I still hadn't left the hospital. Thankfully I was rarely alone as my tight-knit circle enfolded me. I gained solace in their nearness. I also gained strength from the prayers around the world for my girl. Her story had gone viral, and people wanting updates on my daughter were now reading the blog I had started for updates on Joel's cancer journey. I was receiving prayers and well wishes from all parts of the world. I heard from people in England, Australia, even Turkey telling me they had wept and prayed for my daughter's life. Stories were also so graciously sent to me of other children recovering from meningitis and going on to live a full life. I clung to those prayers and stories with all I had. They were the lifeline in the midst of some very rough seas.

Ellis had gotten to the point where she had stabilized a bit, and we had begun to talk about weaning her off her sedation to see where we stood. Only we never got that far. The first indication something was wrong was the intensifying seizures. Of course, since she was sedated, I still couldn't see them as they happened. But the EEG was showing several occurrences within an hour. She also had some labs drawn that were concerning.

Early that morning they decided to take her back for another CT scan to see where we were. I sat in the room alone, waiting for them to bring her back and anxious for the results. Two hours later a doctor appeared in the room and asked to speak with me. She directed me over to a computer screen, where she wanted to show me the CT results as she spoke. I knew from prior experience this did not mean anything good.

"So we got the results of the CT. It is not good news," she said bluntly.

I braced myself for what was coming next.

"It appears the swelling has increased significantly. There are many areas of the brain that are now dead. It also appears she has had several ischemic strokes," she said.

Ischemic strokes. The same exact stroke her daddy had suffered. Just one of those strokes had rendered him paralyzed completely on one side of his body. She hadn't just had one stroke—she'd had several. The pain was so real I felt like I was being stabbed in the chest.

"What are your expectations for Ellis if she comes off the vent?" she asked.

My mind was a mess, my thoughts incoherent.

"I. . .I, well, I don't know," I stammered, at a loss.

"Well, I will tell you what my expectations are," she offered. "If she is ever able to come off the vent, she will never be as she was. She will most likely be in a vegetative state, not able to give or receive affection. Basic function such as walking, talking, et cetera, she will never be able to do. It might be best to start to consider your options," she said, delivering the final blow.

I sat there in total shock, trying desperately to even form a sentence.

"Okay," was all I could muster.

"Do you have any questions for me?" she asked.

"No. No, I don't," I responded.

"If you change your mind, please feel free to have your nurse come get me," she finished.

She left the room, and I started to slowly unravel. There was no more hope for my baby girl. She was dying. Unless God radically intervened, she was going to die. I had just said good-bye to my husband. Now I was going to have to say good-bye to her, too? Two funerals in less than two years? It was inconceivable.

I lay down on my bed and curled into the tightest ball I possibly could and started to sob. I couldn't stop. Every emotion, every fear, every bit of anger was coming to the surface. Every ounce of what I had held inside for the last sixteen months was pouring out in the rawest form during this time at the hospital.

My girlfriend came in for a visit and found me in that state. I was crying so hard I couldn't even talk to her. She sat on my bed rubbing my back as the sobs came harder and harder. I pulled the sheets over my head, trying, in vain, to give myself some privacy from the medical staff coming in and out of the room.

No, no, no, no, no. I can't lose her, I thought. *Please, God, don't let her go. I just got her. I don't want her to go. No, no, no, no. Please. Please.*

The room started to slowly fill with my closest girlfriends—each hearing about my despondency and coming to support me. Some gathered around Ellis's bed to pray over her, and some gathered around to pray for me. Everyone seemed to sense the hole I was in, and no one tried to bring me out of it. I stayed in that place all day long. Hour upon hour I did not move from that bed. I did not eat or drink. I wept from a primal place within me. Four weeks ago this girl was in my belly. Now she was in a hospital bed dying. My arms hadn't held my daughter for two weeks. I ached for her. I didn't want to tell her good-bye. I wasn't ready. This could not be reality.

I wanted to know what her laugh sounded like. I wanted to see her take her first steps. I wanted to know what color her eyes would be. I wanted to hear her say

Mommy. I wanted to see what baby food she would spit out. I wanted to know what her favorite toy was. I was just at the beginning of starting to know her. How could she already leave us?

Why would God give us this miracle baby only to have her taken away? The conversation with Joel in rehab, the dream of her name, the miracle of her life, was it all for nothing? Why was He allowing this to happen? We had been through enough. None of this was making any sense. Would God save her life? Was the woman in the lobby right that this baby would be all right? It was all so hard to understand, and my head was spinning from trying. I wanted to believe, but with each moment my hope was rapidly fading.

The day wore on as I cried and prayed, cried and prayed. I begged God to save her life. Never before have I felt so broken, so desperate. I was surrounded by a crowd of people, yet never before had I felt so alone.

God, please save my baby girl. I'm not ready to let her go.

Two days later the hospital staff asked me if I had made any decisions about how I wished to proceed. By that point in time Ellis had stopped initiating breaths along with her ventilator. They had started to pull her out of some of the sedation. The seizures were now violent and visible every few minutes. Things were looking more and more dire. I didn't know how much more I could take. I kept waiting for a turnaround or some type of miracle to take place, but it never came.

I asked them for one more test, an MRI, to get one last picture of where things stood. I told them after that I would make my final decision. They agreed and took her down for the two-hour test. An hour later two doctors appeared in her doorway, ready to discuss the results.

"It's even worse than we originally thought," the doctor started in.

They went on to show me the pictures and explain the damage. The showed me all the dark spots on her brain that were "dead." They showed me the blood clots and the holes in her brain. They showed me the swelling and where the strokes had occurred. They showed me the inflammation that was still ravaging her brain.

As they spoke the tears slipped down my cheeks. I knew what this meant. I was going to have to let her go.

"I never even knew of this disease," I told them. "I never knew it was something I would ever have to worry about."

"Most people haven't," she replied.

The finality of the moment hit me hard. This was it. I had prayed for a change in her condition, and it had only weakened. My tears dried up. I was too numb to cry anymore.

"I'm sorry. I really am. I'm so sorry," the neurologist said as she left the room.

⁓

An hour later I informed the staff of my decision. The time had come. I would remove Ellis from her vent the next morning. They asked me if I wanted the nurse to help me create some keepsakes. I said yes. I remembered my last few hours with Joel. Never had I expected to have to say good-bye. I blindly believed for a miracle up to the last second. So deeply had I believed that in many ways I regretted not savoring those final moments with him to say good-bye. I would not let that happen this time. I would spend this last night with my daughter relishing every moment.

The nurse brought in paint so we could paint her hands and toes, putting her little baby prints on a canvas. As we rolled the beige paint across her hands I was doubled over, tears pouring down my face. It was just a month ago I was delivering Ellis, and they were taking her prints for her birth certificate. How did we get here?

One by one we made canvases for family members. The nurses handed me scissors, and I cut locks of her hair, delicately placing it inside a small plastic baggie.

The only haircut she will ever receive, I thought. I steadied myself to avoid collapsing under the weight of what we were doing. *Take this moment in,* I thought. *It is the last you will have with your daughter.* I willed myself to continue.

Next she brought out a plaster mold to make for me. I took Ellis's sweet hands and firmly pushed them in the mold. Her feet were next. As we finished, I took the mold and sat on the bed, carving her name in the plaster. *Ellis Claire,* it read with a little heart next to it.

I love her name so much. I will never be able to say it in present tense again, I thought in anger.

As difficult a moment as that was, I moved on, committing it all to memory, determined to save every little piece of her that I could. I had what felt like a permanent lump in my throat, my eyes hot and burning from the amount of tears I had shed. This moment felt as if it would be the death of me.

❧

Friends came in and out that evening, some to pray for a miracle, some to tell her good-bye. At the end of the night, I went over to her bed to tell her good night as I always did. Only that night, it was to be her last night on this earth.

I leaned in to kiss her little legs, drenching them with tears in the process. I sang to her every day, and this day would be no different. I ran through all her favorites in my mind, finally settling on one I thought fit the moment the best.

"You are my sunshine, my only sunshine; you make me happy when skies are gray."

I stopped, my voice breaking, took a deep breath, and continued on.

"You'll never know, dear, how much I love you. Please don't take my sunshine away."

CHAPTER 11
Daring to Hope

My head was pounding as I lifted it from my pillow and looked around the room. I had cried and prayed most of the night. My body had finally succumbed to sleep, only to wake up an hour later as rays of sunlight pierced the room. It was the day.

Everything within me wanted to stay in bed and curl up in a ball. I didn't want to face what I had to do. Who would? All night long I had tried to remember every sweet memory I had of my girl before she was put on the vent. I only had two weeks of them. Not nearly enough. I also tried to think of what I would do for a funeral. How do you even have a funeral for a baby? How do you make sure her life and its impact is not forgotten? How would I tell my two-year-old, who had just lost his father, that he had now lost his sister? It was beyond comprehension.

As intense as those questions were, they took a backseat to something even worse: the guilt. Guilt that this was all somehow my fault. If only I hadn't made the choice to have Ellis, none of this would have happened.

If only I had had her on a different day, maybe she wouldn't have contracted this sickness. If only I had gotten her to the hospital a little earlier that morning, they could have maybe done more for her. On and on it went. Unrelenting.

I stumbled out of bed to the sink, splashing water on my face to try to alert my senses. I turned and walked toward the wall, doing what I had done a thousand times in the weeks before: put antibacterial gel on my hands before I touched her. Even though she had wires poking out of her entire body, she still looked beautiful as ever. In fact, after two weeks of being in the hospital, she looked like she had grown a little.

Today was my little girl's one-month birthday. I would tell her good-bye, only thirty days after I had met her. The thought made me sick to my stomach.

I walked over to the bed and for the first time took down every rail that separated me from her. Before I had been too scared to do so, not wanting to disturb anything. Today I didn't care. I had three hours left until we were removing her from the machine breathing life into her, and I would spend every moment as close to her as I could.

My arms couldn't do much but touch her arm and a leg. I stroked them continually, rested my head beside her face, and told her how much I loved her. Even as I did, seizures were still shaking her entire body every few minutes. As miserable as it would be to say good-bye, I also wanted her to no longer suffer. It seemed my misery would be her gift, the gift of freedom from this painful shell of her body.

Throughout the morning everyone started to arrive. My parents would be in the room when the machines were turned off, as would Lauren and Julie, two of the same girlfriends who had been in the room when I said good-bye to Joel. Outside the PICU was more family in the waiting room and even more friends pacing the hall in prayer.

The evening before I had spoken with the medical staff and given them very clear instructions on how I wanted this to happen. I had thought long and hard about how I wished to say good-bye, and the details were important to me. First of all, I wanted to hold her skin to skin. This was the way she had entered the world, and this would be the way she would leave it. They were to unhook her from the vent, every wire, and place her directly on my chest. The only wire remaining would be a small one attached to her toe. This was so they could monitor her vitals from the desk outside the room and come in to tell us when she had passed. I wanted to sit in the rocking chair in the far corner of the room and read her first story to her. After a long debate, we took the advice of the medical staff and decided she would have one shot of morphine to help with the pain and make her passing as peaceful as possible. I hoped it would be quick, without any further suffering.

I also asked my parents to take all my belongings from the past two weeks to the car so I could leave the hospital as soon as it was all over. Soon, it would sadly all be over.

It was five minutes before the doctor was to arrive to start the process. The nurse came over and touched me on the shoulder.

"I am going to change her diaper one last time. Would you like to do it?"

I didn't want to have any regrets, so I said yes. As I slowly unbuckled the fasteners on the old diaper, I started to double over, dissolving in tears.

You can do this. You have to do this. Be strong, I told myself.

It was a horrific moment, but if Ellis was going to be having one last anything, I wanted to be the one doing it.

It took much longer than it should have, the tears clouding my eyes as I wept through the entire process. My mind raced back to the late-night diaper changes two weeks prior. What I wouldn't give to have every single one of those moments back.

The time finally arrived, and everyone took their place:

my friends and family in the far corner across from me, praying fervently and hoping for a miracle. I ducked into the bathroom for a quick moment to put on the hospital gown I would be wearing, giving the hospital staff easy access to place Ellis on my chest.

As I was undressing, it struck me how everyone so desperately believed she would live as I was preparing to say good-bye. I wanted to be as full of faith as they were, but I no longer had it in me. I had believed so deeply for Joel's miracle that I didn't feel as if I savored my good-bye with him. I didn't want that to happen with my daughter. God had many opportunities in the past two weeks to give us a miracle, and He hadn't. I had no reason to believe it would happen now at the eleventh hour. Yet still, even as little faith as I had left, I still had that tiny mustard seed of belief He could do the impossible.

"God," I whispered quietly in the tiny bathroom, "if there is any way, any way at all You can, please heal her. Thirty days is not enough."

That moment revealed something deep within me, for as much as I thought my faith was all but gone, the core essence of who I was is one who still, against all odds, believed. At that point I didn't believe He would, but I knew He could, and though I had exhausted myself in asking before, I still had to ask one last time.

I opened the bathroom door and entered the room.

The doctor and nurse were surrounding Ellis's bed waiting to begin. I took my seat in the rocking chair and waited.

It seemed as if everyone in the room was holding their breath. Thirty seconds later she was in my arms, her little warm body snuggled against my chest—my first time to hold her in weeks. No wires or cords we in our way; it felt so right, as it should have been all along. Only this would be the last time my arms would ever hold her. There were a million things I wanted to say to her in that moment, but I also knew the time would most likely be short as they had told us earlier she would most likely pass in minutes.

"Ellis, I am so, so proud of you, baby girl. You fought so hard. You are a brave little one," I said through tears. "I want you to know that it's okay to go. Don't be afraid. Soon you will be with Jesus, and with your daddy. I am a little jealous."

I stopped for a moment, and then went on, rocking her back and forth as I spoke. She was quiet and still.

"You will get to meet your sibling. I never knew if it was a little boy or a little girl. I always thought it was a boy, but today you will know. They will take good care of you until I see you again, my love."

The words were coming out in sobbing, broken gasps, but I had to continue.

"I will miss you so much. I wish I could go with you,

but I can't. Your brother and I have to stay here a little longer. We will be there before you know it, but oh, how we will miss you," I told her. "You are the most beautiful girl I have ever seen, Ellis Claire, and I am so proud to be your mommy, so proud. I love you, my sweet girl. I love you."

I had said what I wanted to say, and now it was time to read to her. I quickly grabbed the book, wanting to dive in before she took her last breath, which felt like it could come at any moment. The book I had chosen was *On the Night You Were Born* by Nancy Tillman. This was the same poignant book Milo and I read together the night before her arrival. Those were simple times of eager anticipation of what was to be. How would I have ever known it would come to this?

I opened the book and began, the first and last book I would ever read to my child. I read each line of the book as if it were written especially for her. In that moment it felt as if it was. For her birth had changed our lives forever, and her death would do the same.

As I finished the story, it happened. She let out a loud cry. I gasped. I didn't think I would ever hear her voice again. It seemed like a gift, the chance to hear it one last time. I pulled her in and held her even closer, wanting her to feel every bit of love and security my arms could provide.

I rocked her back and forth, talking to her, singing to her, trying to commit each moment to memory. The rest of the room was silent the entire time, each in his or her own thoughts and headspace.

She was so still and hadn't seized once. I kept waiting to feel the shift in the room when her spirit left her body, as I had with her father. I had no idea how much time had passed, but it began to seem like it had been a lot, certainly not just minutes. If she had passed away I didn't *feel* it happen, but I also wasn't feeling much movement that indicated she was still with us, either.

I looked over at my dad and called him to my side.

"Dad, would you please go out to the desk where they are monitoring her and tell me if she has passed?" I asked.

He nodded quietly and said okay. Moments later he reappeared. I looked at him expecting a sad nod in the affirmative, that our little girl was gone. He didn't do that.

He walked over and bent down beside me.

"Sarah, I talked to them. Ellis is still alive. In fact, they said her pulse ox is good. She is breathing well. Not only that, they said her heart rate is steady and so are all her vitals."

I was stunned. What on earth was happening? They told me she didn't have enough brain function to continue breathing. She had completely stopped even trying to breathe with her vent. Why was she breathing now? I didn't know what was going on, but I assumed I would still be saying good-bye to my girl today. There was nothing more I could do in the moment, so we continued to rock.

Another long stretch of time seemed to pass, but it was just another hour. Again, I was waiting for her shift from this earth but not sensing it had happened. I sent my dad back out to the desk to check on her vitals once again. This time he came back in the room grinning as he announced to our entire room Ellis was still holding strong and improving each minute. A shift was now taking place in the room, but it was not with Ellis—it was with us. I watched as the worried faces of my friends and family started to relax into smiles. I was desperate for her to live but still not so sure she would.

"Lord," I asked, "do I dare to hope?"

I wanted to. I wanted to believe the God of the miraculous was giving us a miracle for my Ellis. Yet, I had believed so many times in the past. Years and years of belief that came crashing down in a horrific ending. I wasn't quite ready to believe again.

I continued to rock my girl as she slowly began to become more aware. Another cry from her pierced the air, then another, each one filling her lungs with breath again. I started to feel them now on my chest, small breath in and small breath out. She was doing it. She had stopped breathing on the machine, but she was doing it on her own. She had been on massive amounts of medications that still wouldn't control her vitals, yet now without any medicines her body was controlling them on her own. She'd had endless amounts of seizures, yet once she was in my arms, they had completely stopped. It was as if my embrace was all she needed all along. It seemed impossible. It was impossible. Simply put, a miracle.

Time ticked on, hour after hour, and she wasn't getting weaker—she was getting stronger. My dad would check in each hour, and it was incredible to be told the same thing: she was still alive. Four hours in, he left the room and came back with the doctor.

"Well," she started in, "I don't know what to say. She's a fighter."

I smiled. "Yes, she is."

"At this point we don't really know if she will pass or if she will live. We just don't know," she said.

She was perplexed. I could tell. We all were.

"We will keep an eye on you through the night, and if she continues on this road, we will release you into a room on the floor." She didn't say much more but didn't need to. With each hour, what was happening was becoming clear. At the eleventh hour, when her life was all but gone, we were getting our miracle. My prayers were not hitting the ceiling but the very throne room of God. He heard. He answered.

Hope was rising and joy was exploding with each person in that room. We knew we were witnessing a miracle. As time moved forward, it became more concrete. Ellis Claire was going to live.

"I can't believe it," I said in tears over and over again. "I just can't believe it."

I wished Joel were here to witness this moment. Without his life there wouldn't be an Ellis. His life was not healed on this earth, but in heaven he was whole. Yet his daughter's life would be healed here, right before my eyes. Their names both meant the same thing—"Jehovah is God." Their lives each declared that fact in uniquely different ways, both in life and death. Yes, miracles didn't happen when I thought they would come, but they did happen when I no longer believed they could.

None of it made any sense, but in that moment, I didn't need the answer to my whys. I just needed to hold on to my baby girl and soak in every moment.

❧

We were now nine hours in, and my friends finally convinced me to eat something. Ellis was snuggled deeply into my chest, not moving an inch. The plan was to keep her that way until further notice. She was breathing resolutely, but she was still so delicate in my arms, limp from not moving a muscle for half her life. Friends and family were coming in and out of the room, wanting to get a peek at Ellis, not even believing the miracle that was unfolding right before their eyes.

Things started to wind down around 8:00 that evening, and after a long day, most everyone had gone. It was time to get some much-needed sleep on my trusty hospital futon. They propped me up with pillows all around, so I could sleep with her on my chest. It had been so long since my arms had held my baby girl; I never wanted to let her go. A mere nine hours prior I was telling her good-bye, yet now I was reacquainting myself with a life I thought I would never have the chance to know.

The next morning the doctor came to tell me that they were releasing us from the PICU and onto the regular floor. I asked for a wheelchair so I could continue to hold Ellis to my chest. By that time we were twenty-six hours in and I had not let her go, except for a single one-minute bathroom break. My request was granted, and before I knew it we were both being wheeled out of the unit that had been our home for two long weeks. Nurses gathered around to tell us good-bye, many with perplexed looks on their faces, not quite knowing how to respond to this baby girl.

Once we reached the floor, the transition was jarring. Ellis went from monitors continually keeping track of every vital sign to check-ins every four hours.

Nurses who had been in and out of the room every few moments now had to be called into the room at our request. I realized I had left a cocoon of sorts, and the real work for me would now begin. I was scared—scared that I would do something wrong and hurt her, scared that I wouldn't be able to take care of her, scared for what was in store and what her future held. This was all uncharted territory, not only for me but for the medical staff as well.

Yet as time moved forward, I couldn't help but believe that the work the Lord had started would be finished. I only had my trusty mustard seed, but in the end, it was all I needed for mountains to move. I didn't have all the answers as to how our future would play out, but I was growing more resolute each day as our new life together in the hospital passed.

Three days in I decided the time had finally come to release Ellis from my arms and let someone else hold her. I was in desperate need of a shower and felt like she was stable enough to let someone else hold her. Something told me that for the rest of her life letting go was going to be hard with her, but if there is one person I can trust with my daughter, it is the One who loves her even more than I.

That afternoon was filled with different pediatricians coming in to see her and developing a plan for when we went home. They were being cautiously optimistic, more comfortable with telling me all the things that could go wrong while I told them over and over again she would defy the odds.

She had her first chance to show off that afternoon. Since she was off her feeding tube, we had to discuss how she would get her nutrition. Doctors wanted to go ahead and put a feeding tube in her while I wanted to see if she would take a bottle. They told me to brace myself—that her being able to take a bottle was highly unlikely. According to the scans and the assumed damage to her brain, she likely wouldn't have the skills required to do so. I was adamant they let her try. They sent in a speech pathologist, who came in to delicately walk us through the process.

"Now, we are going to give this a try," she said. "Maybe we can get her to take a tiny bit, but we just won't know until we try."

My mom did the honor of holding the bottle up to Ellis's lips and then putting it inside her mouth. I held my breath. Ellis began to suck away.

"Oh wow. Wow," the pathologist said. "Whoa there, little one, slow down."

Ellis drank the bottle so quickly we had to stop her so her delicate tummy wouldn't throw it all back up. They had told us previously if Ellis did live, there would likely be no way she would leave the hospital without a trach tube to help her breathe and a feeding tube to help her eat. It was now apparent she would leave with neither.

∽

The next day was another long-awaited moment when Milo finally got to see his baby sister. He had fallen in love with her instantly the day she was born, only to have her and me suddenly disappear from his life for three weeks. I knew it had been hard on him, but I never wanted him to see her in that condition. There are some things a child should never see.

My parents brought him up to the hospital that evening, and he slowly walked in the room. His eyes locked in on me holding her, and a big smile spread across his face.

"Is that my baby sister?" he wondered aloud.

"Yes, buddy, it is," I said.

"Are you feeding her a bottle?" he asked.

"I am. Isn't that so neat that she can take a bottle?" I asked him.

He nodded enthusiastically, not even grasping a tenth of how amazing it was.

"Is she all better now?" he asked me in his sweet baby voice.

"Yes, bubs, Mommy and baby sister get to come home very soon because she is doing much, much better," I said with a smile.

"I just think that she needed her Milo," he replied confidently.

The room erupted in laughter as I ran my fingers through his hair and kissed his forehead.

"You know what? I think you're right. I think her Milo is exactly what she needed," I agreed.

I looked back and forth at my two children, who I never thought would be together again, and once again felt as if my heart would explode. I knew I was not only looking at one miracle but two. Two little ones entrusted to us, as the greatest gift I had ever received.

◦◦

The following morning I removed Ellis's little hat to check on her head swelling and noticed it had gone down by about 80 percent in only a few days' time. Her brain swell, which had only gotten worse each day she was in the PICU, had now reversed and was going in the opposite direction. The miracle was continuing.

As the day went on, we started to have several visitors—only they were doctors and nurses from the PICU staff. Many of them had seen Ellis in her worst state. They knew what her scans said. They knew she shouldn't be alive. They couldn't believe what their eyes were seeing any more than we could.

"We just wanted to come by and take a quick peek at

Ellis. Is that okay?" a couple of residents asked timidly.

"Of course," I said.

"Wow, she looks like she is doing so well," one of them said.

"She is, she is doing perfectly," I responded.

"We heard she took a bottle. Is that true?" they asked.

"She did. She has been sucking them down like there's no tomorrow," I said.

They both shook their heads in unison.

"Aren't you glad almost everything we told you was wrong?" one of them asked.

"You have no idea just how glad," I answered with a smile.

❧

We had now been on the main floor for five days and were set to be released in two. A palliative care doctor came in and went over everything I needed to know for our release the following morning. Out of an abundance of caution, they were sending us home with hospice care. It was not with the intention that she would die; it was more the intention that she needed an extra set of medical eyes watching over her as she first returned home. I listened as line by line the doctor told me the worst-case scenarios as to what to look out for in case things started to go terribly wrong.

"The goal would obviously be for Ellis to get strong

enough to be discharged from hospice, but we just don't know, you know, how things will turn out," she told me.

"Well, I am hopeful," I told her.

"You know Ellis is about a one in a million baby," she said. "Her scans were. . ."—she paused—"incompatible with life."

"I know she is," I said in return. "Listen, Doctor, I don't understand any of this any more than you do. But I know this: I know my baby girl is a miracle. And I don't know what our future holds, but I have a strong feeling that this little girl is going to continue to astound," I said.

She let out a slight smile, nodding slowly.

"I. . .I think that, too," she finally relented.

The next morning the moment had come; it was time to go home. I hurried around the room, packing up all the things I had amassed over my nearly monthlong stay in the hospital. I changed Ellis into the first outfit she had worn in weeks and delicately loaded her up in her car seat. My mom arrived to collect all our things, taking them down to the car in multiple trips. The nurse came with all our prescriptions and permission to head out the door. Just as I had when we left the hospital after her birth, I placed Ellis in her car seat in my lap as my mom wheeled me out of the hospital. This seemed like a rebirth, a take two. Life had taken us to the darkest places, and by a miracle of the

Lord, we got the chance to start over again. Not every family got to leave the children's hospital with their child in their arms. Our life came incredibly close to that same outcome. That thought made me all the more thankful as I held Ellis close.

We loaded her up in her car seat as she wailed with her disapproval. At one point in life I would have maybe tried to quiet her, but now I loved to hear her scream. It meant she was alive, something I would never again take for granted.

As we pulled into the driveway, I looked at my house and was flooded with relief, excited to finally be home. We walked in the front door as Milo ran to tackle me, squealing with delight.

"Can I hold her?" he asked excitedly.

"Of course you can," I told him.

By that point she had quieted down and finally faded off to sleep. I gingerly reached in to pull her out and put her on the pillow in her brother's lap. He held her tenderly, looking at her face with wonderment.

Life had taken us to some incredible places. I thought back on the beginning of a journey that started with an "I do," a promise of a forever love, which would remain a forever love. It had led us down the path of infertility, which handed us a loss, yet two joyous births. I thought about the day I told my husband good-bye, but how his life continues to inspire and direct our family to this day. I thought about the moment I let Ellis go, only to have her miraculously returned back to my life, to our life. Life—it is a funny thing, filled with much heartbreak, yet in this moment deep wells of joy, ashes to beauty and so much more.

"Mommy," Milo said, interrupting my thoughts, "you're home."

"Yes, buddy, you are right." I thought, *If only he knew in more ways than one.* "We are. We are home."

Epilogue

S arah, she is perfect," the nurse said with a smile.

What every mom wants to hear. It had been three months since Ellis had been released from the hospital, and she was doing incredibly well. She had slowly been gaining the weight back she lost in the hospital and then some. She was now double the size that she was. The swelling in her head had completely gone away. After she got off the vent, she never again had another seizure. She had three different doctor's appointments in the weeks prior, each doctor confirming her progress and what a miracle she continued to be. One even said she was "laughing in the face of medicine." That's my girl.

"Really?" I asked. "You really think she's perfect?"

"Sarah, I see no signs at all of brain damage in this child," she said. An amazing statement considering all Ellis had been through. "I think if you put her in a lineup with other babies her age, no one would know the difference."

I looked down at Ellis in my arms as she smiled and cooed in approval. It was amazing how far she had come in such a short time.

"The only sad thing is we are going to have to work on getting her discharged," she responded.

Discharged. The words I had been waiting to hear. Ellis was doing so well she no longer needed hospice to monitor her.

"It came so quick," I told the nurse. "It seems like just the other day was your first time you came to see her."

"I know," she responded. "She was so little and fragile. Now she seems like a completely different child. I am going to miss this little baby girl."

"The doctor did say she is one in a million," I said with a chuckle.

"One in a million?" she said. "I would say more like one in a hundred million."

We both looked at Ellis and laughed at this little one who continued to astound.

I walked the nurse to the door and gave her a hug good-bye, promising to let her still stop by and see Ellis as she grew.

Just then Ellis let out a big yawn—it was time for her nap. I walked her back to her bedroom to put her in her crib, laying her right underneath the big sign that adorned her wall.

WHEN SHE WAKES, SHE WILL MOVE MOUNTAINS, it read.

I smiled as I watched her drift off to sleep, completely unaware of the mountains already bowing at her feet.

❧

A few months later, I was in the guest room of a very special place packing my bag, with tears streaming down my face—only these were the good kind of tears. I had just spent the weekend at a retreat for ones who have walked through trauma and want to see their lives healed and whole. Oh, how I wanted to live a life healed and whole. This brief time away was the first step toward it.

The retreat was just what I needed—a weekend of remembering where I have been yet building hope again for my future. My first day there I noticed a painting on the wall, a beautiful, vibrant bouquet of flowers. I felt the Lord softly whisper to my heart, *I want to see you bloom again.* Bloom. Hope. Dream. All the things that were at the core of who I was, before tragedy came and momentarily took it all away.

New beginnings have abounded for me and my family. I left the career I had built for the previous eight years. I was never passionate about my job. Losing Joel made me realize how short life is, and I didn't want to live another minute seeking only provision. I wanted my heart to sing again. I wanted to soar. I have found that in many ways through words—through sharing with many blog readers who have faithfully followed our story. To see lives changed through our story is just icing on the cake.

Milo continues to blossom. My first miracle baby, the one who made me a mom, is a full-on big boy now. The essence of who his father was is so deeply carried in the heart of my son. He talks about Daddy all the time. He knows who his father is and how completely he loved his boy. We make Joel a part of our day, every day. Whenever I really miss my husband, I need look no further than our Milo, who is the spitting image of him in just about every way.

Then there's Ellis. Well, she was just born to shine. Her life continues to astound as she scales every wall they said she would never climb. She is full of joy and loves to laugh and sing. She is always hitting new milestones each month—sitting up, rolling over, laughing, giving kisses, saying several words including (my favorite one) "Mama," and most recently starting to stand. She has also begun to initiate steps, and her therapists believe walking is right around the corner. Each are things we thought she might never accomplish, and we rejoice at her divine progress. Her story has traveled the world and back again. She has been on the front page of newspapers and featured on television. Each time they talk about the miraculous way her life was saved and the goodness and faithfulness of our God. The mountains continue to move.

You never move on, but you can move forward. The

best way to honor my husband's life is to do just that. Keep moving. Keep running our race well. The Choose Joy Project is a testament to that and continues annually in remembrance of him. That's how we honor his legacy. By refusing to bow in defeat. By choosing to rise.

Not a day goes by that I don't miss my husband, my sweet JoJo. It has not been easy living this life without him. But as I grieve, I grieve with hope for the moment when we will see him again and when all things will be made new. Hope in the promise that we will continue to see beauty rise from our ashes and redemption birthed from our pain; trusting that the Author of our story will write its glorious ending.

I finished up packing my belongings and began to wheel my suitcase to the door leading to a new path before me. I gave my counselor one last hug as the tears rolled down my cheeks. My life was changed. My heart felt whole again. It was not as if I had forgotten where I had come from. Never. But I have started to anticipate where we would be and what the Lord has in store for our little family. Through the darkest hour of our lives, He was there. He wept with us. He held us in our pain. He mourned with us in our grief. Now He was steadying my heart and gently leading me forward.

I said my good-byes and made my way to the lobby. Here I was, once again, about to embark on another adventure—the adventure of life. No one ever knows what's in store, but I can now face it with confidence—confidence in who I am, confidence in who walks beside me. I am never alone. I was never alone.

A smile slowly crept across my face. Peace washed over me. As I gently turned the knob to what awaited me, sunshine broke through, bathing me in the most magnificent light. We were going to be okay. We were going to be okay.

With that, I took a deep breath and slowly but surely walked out the door.

About the Author

Sarah Rodriguez is a graduate of Victory Bible College in Tulsa and currently resides in Oklahoma. She is a writer and speaker and is active in her church community through worship and other avenues of serving. She was blessed to be married to her husband, Joel, for eight incredible years. She is Mommy to Milo and Ellis.

Visit Sarah's blog: http://journeyofsarah.com/

For more information on the Choose Joy Project, visit: http://journeyofsarah.com/choose-joy-project/

Portions of the proceeds from this book will be donated to an organazation near and dear to Sarah's heart—Beads of Good. For more information visit: www.beadsofgood.org.

Discover the Power of Prayer

Power Prayers Devotional

Scripture encourages us to "come boldly unto the throne of grace" (Hebrews 4:16)—and this *Power Prayers Devotional* will help with 180 inspiring prayer starters. These powerful meditations encourage women of all ages and backgrounds to approach God in intimate, joyful, confident prayer. Whenever you say, "Here I am, Lord," He is thrilled to listen to your deepest hopes and fears. Start on your journey of truer, deeper, more effective communion with the Lord who loves you with an everlasting love.

DiCarta / 978-1-61626-608-0 / $14.99

Power Prayers to Start Your Day Devotional Journal

This delightful journal from Barbour Publishing fits perfectly into a woman's prayer life. Journalers will find themselves encouraged and inspired to record all of the ways they are blessed and loved by their heavenly Father. Fabulous as a gift—or for personal use—this journal will be cherished for years to come.

DiCarta / 978-1-63409-636-2 / $17.99

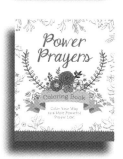

Power Prayers Coloring Book

Color your way to a more powerful prayer life with the brand-new *Power Prayers* coloring book. Forty-five unique images on quality stock will comfort and inspire through beautiful design and refreshing prayers. The backs of each generous 8x10 coloring page are left blank—perfect for coloring with crayons, colored pencils, and markers.

Paperback / 978-1-63409-968-4 / $9.99